The Golden Age of Ivy League Basketball:

from Bill Bradley to Penn's Final Four, (1964-1979)

...with a brief history of Ivy basketb[...]
1897 to Harvard's NCAA Tournament [...]

PAUL A. HUTTER

To Jeremy Lin
Without whose inspiration this book would never have
been started...

...and Bill Cronin
Without whose motivation this book would never have
been completed

Contents

Preface

The following manuscript is a first hand perspective of what the *New York Times* referred to as the post-Bill Bradley Golden Age of Ivy League basketball "when elite universities had elite basketball teams to match". It is an apocryphal, Churchillian and Zelig-like accounting which not only covers the Golden Age years between 1964 and 1979, but also provides a background review for the time-continuum spanning from pre-history cavemen to current NBA leading scorer, Carmelo Anthony (20,000 B.C. to 2013 A.D.). While it might seem far-fetched to suggest that not much has changed over this vast time period, the myriad "six degrees of separation" connections that permeate human history have many strands leading to and emanating from the Golden Age era.

In addition to the historical backstory, specific details regarding Ivy League teams, players, coaches and institutions, as well as the evolution of the media, should both elicit Baby Boomer memories and trigger discussion/ controversy pertaining to "what happened then" and "how we got to now". Finally, in addition to a glorious past, a case can be made that Ivy League basketball has a promising and healthy future—one that has the potential to match or even surpass the memorable Golden Age.

While great drivers of historical narrative such as Winston Churchill or Woody Allen's Zelig can influence our perceptions of the past, in the end, each of us must examine the facts and draw our own conclusions regarding what really happened back in the day. This book represents my researched recollections of the Golden Age era and beyond. While I challenge readers to refute the facts, I also invite alternative recollections and perceptions of this memorable era as others will have their own unique take which differs from my perspective and opinions.

This book is not meant to be a non-fiction polemic or an historical academic treatise. Rather, it is merely a sports handbook/reference book, chock full of nostalgic data, statistics and trivia, which the "classic basketball fan" will hopefully find to be both enjoyable and amusing.

Introduction

The Golden Age of Ivy League basketball is a period that is still redolent in the memory of those born between 1930 and 1965; specifically, the entire Baby Boom generation (1946-1964). Yet, since the onset of the modern era of sports media (ESPN in 1979), the narrative driving the perception of Ivy League basketball is that of highbrow but hapless Davids fighting, against all odds, to slay the power-house Goliaths.

This book punctures that myth, and sets the record straight in explaining that between the time Bill Bradley's iconic Princeton career ended in 1965 and Penn appeared in the 1979 Final Four, the Ivy League was a Goliath, members of which even verged on becoming a basketball dynasty. Between 1964 and 1972 the league was a power conference equal to the ACC or Big 10, stocked with future NBA players and draftees.

In addition to the overriding importance of Bill Bradley to the birth of the Golden Age, the career of Coach Butch van Breda Kolff and his role as "The Father of the Golden Age" is examined in depth. Also, the journey from Goliath (or dynasty as embodied by the February 27, 1967 *Sports Illustrated* cover featuring Princeton's Gary Walters and Chris Thomforde) to David (as promoted by ESPN after serial near upsets during the 1980s and 1990s) is analyzed fully.

Current positive developments suggest that, to a limited extent, the Ivy League could be headed "back to the future." While the Golden Age of Ivy League basketball is behind us, the recent rise of Harvard's and Cornell's prospects as Top 25 programs suggests a new era of healthy competition for tenured basketball aristocrats, Penn and Princeton.

The book also undertakes a broad review of Ivy League basketball history from 1897 to 2013. It contains extensive statistical data analysis and rankings covering such topics as the top 20 teams in Ivy League history, the top 20 players in Ivy League history, Ivy League championship history, NCAA Tournament history and NBA player achievements. Data analysis, rankings and player features are supplemented with pictures, tables and graphs.

Finally, there is an extensive review of the accomplishments of the great coaches in Ivy League history including Princeton's Butch van Breda Kolff and Pete Carril, Columbia's Jack Rohan and Penn's Jack McClosky, Dick Harter, Digger Phelps, Chuck Daly and Fran Dunphy. This book is a homage to a bygone era, but one inhabited by many distinguished sports figures who still resonate today in 2013; an elegiac era when NBA-bound basketball goliaths roamed the Ivy League hardwood.

CHAPTER 1

Defining The Era ... "Basketball Brigadoon"

Distilled to its essence, the Golden Age of Ivy League basketball can be defined as follows:

GAIB = VBK + $BILL x NYTIMES

However, the full backstory is infinitely deeper and wider than this simple and not so elegant equation might imply.

On February 19, 2012, an article ran in *The New York Times* with the headline, "In Ivy League's Golden Age, Elite Universities with Teams to Match." The reference was to the post-Bill Bradley Golden Age of Ivy League basketball accomplishment which lasted from 1964 to 1979. Approximately two weeks later, on March 8, 2012, the same *New York Times* ran an article with the headline, "Harvard Encounters a Rare Subject," referring to Harvard winning its first basketball championship since 1946.

What goes around comes around? Not exactly ... although both articles applaud basketball success at elite Ivy League universities, the real story is the difference in the level of accomplishment and the degree of cultural change and upheaval between the time of Bradley's historic achievements in 1964 and Harvard's historic achievement in 2012.

The years between 2010 and 2012 have witnessed the unlikely mini-renaissance of Ivy League basketball. In 2012, Jeremy Lin, point guard for the New York Knicks, became the biggest national media basketball sensation since Princeton's Bill Bradley in 1964. His unassuming demeanor, self-deprecating style and other-worldly statistical accomplishments provided a brief but much needed shot of adrenaline to New York Knicks fans. In February 2012, Madison Square Garden generated more energy than at any time since the early '70s championship days with Walt Frazier and Earl "the Pearl" Monroe. Lin's Harvard pedigree was certainly a central part of the story which also shed a light on one of the nether regions of basketball lore and history: the Golden Age of Ivy League basketball. This Golden Age spanned from the rise in prominence of Bill Bradley as a transcendent national figure in December 1964, to the University of Pennsylvania's crowning achievement of reaching the NCAA Final Four in March 1979. This was also the same year as the famous Michigan State / Indiana State championship battle between Magic Johnson and Larry Bird.

Ivy League basketball history is both glorious and checkered. In 2010, Cornell University had a tremendous run in reaching the NCAA Tournament Sweet 16 bracket before losing to perennial national power, Kentucky. Cornell ended the season ranked No. 12, the highest Ivy League ranking since Princeton cracked the Top 10 in 1998. Also in 2010, Jeremy Lin was an underestimated star for a nascent Harvard program, which in 2012 reached a Top 25 national ranking and won an Ivy League championship under Coach Tommy Amaker, who played at Duke University. If given institutional support, this current Harvard program appears headed toward a bright and successful future. A future that to a limited extent conjures up memories of the post- Bradley Golden Age.

The period immediately following the Golden Age, which ended in 1979, extends from 1980 to Cornell's Sweet 16 achievement in 2010. This checkered period could be labelled the post- Golden Age or more accurately the Wilderness Years. Similar to Europe's 30 Years War, the 17th Century religious wars that extended from approximately 1618 to the Treaty of Westphalia in 1648, the 1980-2010 period could be described as a monumental battle of "hegemonic stasis" between the once great Golden Age powers, Penn and Princeton.

After Penn's 1979 Final Four loss to Magic Johnson

and Michigan State, Penn and Princeton remained the dominant Ivy League teams during the 1980s and '90s. However, they were no longer significant players on the national stage. 1979 would be the last time that any Ivy League team advanced beyond the second round of the NCAA Tournament until Cornell's Sweet 16 success in 2010. While either Penn or Princeton consistently won the Ivy League title during this 30 year period, their NCAA Tournament appearances were reduced to cameo "one game wonders" highlighted by Princeton's near upset of the top ranked, Alonzo Mourning-led Georgetown team in 1989, as well as Princeton's shocking upset of the defending NCAA Champion, UCLA, in round one of the 1996 tournament.

At the national level there were occasional peek-a-boo forays into the Top 25 rankings with Penn reaching No. 11 in 1995 and the aforementioned Princeton team achieving a Top 10 ranking in 1998. Although the '98 Tigers were unable to reach the Sweet 16 during the NCAA Tournament, this Bill Carmody coached team briefly rekindled a proud air of nostalgia regarding Princeton's historic achievements during the post- Bradley Golden Age. Key 1998 Princeton players included Mitch Henderson and the talented center, Steve Goodrich. Goodrich, who also starred at Penn Charter School in Philadelphia, more recently famous as the alma mater of Atlanta Falcons QB Matt Ryan, even briefly reached the NBA ranks playing for the New Jersey Nets in 2002. His achievement of NBA player status, which has been extremely rare in recent years, was a routine occurrence during the Ivy League's Golden Age.

The Golden Age, while loosely defined as the years between 1964 and 1979, was actually an amalgam of tightly identified periods based on a set of unique dates and accomplishments. Specifically, it was comprised of a discrete and precise beginning, ascendency, peak, decline and ending. Each of these sub-periods possesses its own stars and unique set of anecdotes. These anecdotes run the gamut from internecine team and coaching rivalries to the discussion of "who was Lisa Halaby's (the future Queen Noor of Jordan) basketball team boyfriend and at 6'6", with Brad Pitt features, how he was the polar opposite of King Hussein" ... However, he didn't rule over his own country.

On a cultural and societal level, the U.S. changed dramatically between 1964 and 1979. This period of upheaval spanned the immediate post - John F. Kennedy assassination year, the beginning and end of the Vietnam War, the turbulent years of political unrest on American college campuses, the beginning and end of the "hippie" counter-culture movement, and finally, the impact of the civil rights movement culminating with the assassination of Martin Luther King Jr.

While this swirling stew of societal instability was

unfolding, the cult hero success of Bill Bradley and his coach, Butch van Breda Kolff, was raising the profile of Ivy League basketball to a stature not unlike that of Duke and North Carolina today in 2013.

So, as previously discussed, the post- Bill Bradley Golden Age can be segmented into five distinct component parts:

I.   The Beginning ... December 1964 to March 1965
II. The Ascendency ... March 1965 to May 1969
III. The Peak ... May 1969 to December 1971
IV. The Decline ... December 1971 to March 1979
V.   The Ending ... March 1979

The Beginning

According to Ivy League basketball scripture, it is accepted wisdom that "in the beginning there was Bill Bradley." However, this is not altogether true because without the great coach, Butch van Breda Kolff, there would be no Bill Bradley, at least as he came to be known: demigod, transformational legend, Rhodes Scholar, future president (or at least senator) and role model for all baby boomer boys with a modicum of academic and athletic prowess. Finally, and most important for the Ivy League's Golden Age, he became a role model for academically and athletically talented high school All-American basketball recruits with aspirations of playing in the NBA ... and if they didn't make it to the NBA, their fallback position might be to become a doctor, lawyer, corporate executive, venture capitalist, Wall Street analyst, etc.

Butch van Breda Kolff was a genius coach who leveraged Bradley's star power to recruit a group of talented high school stars including Gary Walters, Ed Hummer, and Robbie Brown. His fast-paced, NBA-style game led Princeton to a record of 103-31 and four Ivy League championships between 1962 and 1967. After Princeton he became the coach of an excellent Los Angeles Lakers team anchored by Wilt Chamberlain and Jerry West. His Lakers lost in the NBA Finals in 1968 and 1969 to the Bill Russell-led Boston Celtics. However, it was between 1962 and 1965 that van Breda Kolff, in mentoring and honing Bradley's game, laid the foundation for the Ivy League's Golden Age, which began in December 1964 with an epic battle at the sports world's most prestigious venue.

The 1964 Holiday Festival Tournament championship game was between Princeton and No. 1 ranked Michigan, led by 6'6" All-American Cazzie Russell. By his senior year the 6'5" Bradley had established himself as the nation's top player and was already a legend. However, to become a true cultural icon it would be necessary to participate in an existential battle between the preternatural "irresistible force and immovable object" on the world stage. That is what this highly anticipated match was between Princeton with Bradley and Michigan led by Russell. It was Ali versus Frazier on the hardwood of Madison Square Garden.

Michigan was a heavy favorite but the question among fans and, in particular, the New York and national press which were instrumental in creating "Bradleymania" (think "Linsanity" pre-ESPN), was whether Bradley was so individually superior that even a stronger Michigan team with its own 1st team All-American could not stop him? Princeton had a solid first half and managed to take a 39-37 halftime lead. Bradley's dominance was undeniable in the second half as Princeton built a 12 point lead with only 4 minutes to go. However, Bradley then fouled out and his undermanned teammates could not protect the lead, losing 80-78. Despite the disappointment, Bradley's reputation was further burnished as he scored 41 points and secured his stature as the nation's best college player since the great Oscar Robertson in 1960.

Even in a loss the national media trumpeted its clarion call that "Dollar Bill' was indeed tantamount to the second coming ... at least in basketball terms. The remainder of Bradley's senior season went about as expected with Princeton winning another Ivy League title and entering the NCAA Tournament with considerable momentum. Several wins and even a visit to the Eastern Regional Finals (equivalent of today's Elite 8) was not out of the question. However, Bradley surpassed expectations, not just once but two times.

First, Bradley and his young supporting cast routed No. 4 ranked Providence in the Eastern Regional, 109-69, to make it to the Final Four. Then, after losing a rematch to Michigan, Bradley finished his fabled college career with a super-human effort scoring 58 points in the consolation game against Wichita State and its All-American, Dave Stallworth. Even in 2013, this remains the highest single-game scoring total in NCAA Tournament history. Again, the national media were doing backflips and spouting superlatives regarding his feats and the media's attention was about to turn to the probability of Bradley becoming the New York Knicks first round draft pick. Little did the press know that Bradley would again confound expectations by forgoing his rookie season to become a Rhodes Scholar at the University of Oxford in England ... you can always tell a Princeton man, you just can't tell him much.

The Ascendancy

Between Bradley's sterling 1965 Final Four appearance and the distribution of freshman admission notices on April 15, 1969, Ivy League campuses became a veritable turnstile of top high school All-American recruits. Among them were Geoff Petrie, John Hummer and Chris Thomforde at Princeton; Jim McMillian and Hayward Dotson at Columbia and Steve Bilsky, Dave Wohl and

Corky Calhoun at Penn. These three schools were now established, nationally-ranked programs with expectations of attracting top talent. However, the apex of the Golden Age occurred when Harvard of all places, a football and ice hockey factory from somewhere near Canada, had its own recruiting coup by signing high school All-Americans, James Brown and Floyd Lewis; thus, drawing the battle lines for competition with Penn, Princeton and Columbia ... the boys from up north meant business!

The Peak

In May of 1969 James Brown, who went on to fame as the ubiquitous football anchor for CBS Sports, decided to enroll at Harvard. Brown was the star at DeMatha High School, probably the most famous and historic program in the country. It was DeMatha, coached by Morgan Wootten, that in 1965 defeated the unbeatable New York City Power Memorial team and its superstar Lew Alcindor, later to become Kareem Abdul- Jabaar. Even today, DeMatha is still consistently listed among the top high school powers in *USA Today*'s national rankings.

Also in April of 1969, high school All-Americans and future NBA players Brian Taylor and Ted Manakas were admitted to Princeton while future NBA player Phil Hankinson was admitted to Penn. These talented players, many of whom might opt for Duke or Stanford today, represented the high water mark for post-Bradley, NBA-caliber recruiting.

Between May 1969 and March 1972, the Ivy League remained among the top basketball conferences in the country. The great UCLA dynasty notwithstanding, the Ivy League was arguably on par with the Atlantic Coast Conference (Duke and North Carolina) and the Big 10 (Michigan and Indiana). Therefore, it was fitting then that the peak of the Ivy League's national prominence was reached on December 6, 1971 with a victory by Princeton over No. 2 ranked North Carolina at Princeton's Jadwin Gym. Similar to Princeton's 1964 clash with Michigan and Penn's 1971 Elite 8 loss to Villanova, this game was highly anticipated. However, unlike those games, Princeton not only came away with the victory but the game was a one-sided affair that clearly demonstrated Ivy League power and prestige.

As one might expect, North Carolina was considered to be the most talented team in the country next to UCLA, which that year was led by Bill Walton and Keith Wilkes. North Carolina's 6'10" Bob McAdoo was the best offensive player in the country and would go on to lead the NBA in scoring several times including a 34 ppg average in 1975. 6'8" Bobby Jones was the top defensive forward in the country and went on to an all-star NBA career which included being a key component of the 1983 NBA Champion Philadelphia 76ers led by Dr. J, Julius Erving, and Moses Malone. The North Carolina point guard was George Karl, who not only had a solid NBA career but also went on to become one of the great coaches in NBA history.

Coach Pete Carril's team was led by 6'2" future NBA star, Brian Taylor, as well as point guard and future NBA player, Ted Manakas. Princeton's 6'11" center, Andy Rimol, had the unenviable task of matching up against McAdoo. Princeton survived an early 6-0 North Carolina spurt to come back and take the halftime lead 36-34. In the second half Princeton's relentless defensive pressure inexorably wore down the vaunted North Carolina offense. By the end, 23 points by Rimol and 21 each by Taylor and Manakas highlighted an 89-73 Princeton rout. This was not an upset ... it was a blowout!

Unbeknownst to everyone in Jadwin Gym that day (including myself) was that we not only had witnessed a great Princeton victory, but also the beginning of the end of the Ivy League's Golden Age. There would be other significant achievements, in particular, Princeton's 1975 NIT championship and Penn's 1979 Final Four appearance, but the great years of Ivy League basketball with NBA-caliber recruits were ending. Again, UCLA notwithstanding, between 1964 and 1972 the Ivy League was as good as any conference in the nation, the ACC and Big 10 included. After 1972, this could no longer be said with conviction.

So how good was Ivy League basketball during the Golden Age ascendency and peak between 1964 and 1972 as well as the full 15 year period ending in 1979? A comparison can be drawn versus the 30 year post-Golden Age Wilderness Years (1980-2010):

15 Year Golden Age (1964-1979)	NBA Level	30 Year Wilderness Years (1980-2010)**
13	NBA players	8
1	Hall of Fame	0
3	All Stars	0
2	Rookies of the Year*	0
1	All Defensive Team	0
5	Champion Starters	0
42	NBA Draftees	13
	NCAA Rankings	
6	Top 5	0
9	Top 10	1
15	Top 25	3
	NCAA Tournament	
2	Final 4	0
5	Elite 8	0
7	Sweet 16	0
1	NIT Championships	0

*   Brian Taylor was Rookie of the Year for the ABA New York Nets

**   Years between Penn's Final Four and Cornell's Sweet 16

NBA Players	
15 Year Golden Age	**30 Year Wilderness Years**
Bill Bradley, Princeton (Knicks)	Chris Dudley, Yale (Trailblazers)
Geoff Petrie, Princeton (Trailblazers)	Butch Graves, Yale (Cavaliers)
John Hummer, Princeton (Braves/Clippers)	Matt Maloney, Penn (Rockets)
Brian Taylor, Princeton (Nets)	Steve Goodrich, Princeton (Nets)
Ted Manakas, Princeton (Kings)	Walt Palmer, Dartmouth (Jazz)
Armond Hill, Princeton (Hawks)	Jerome Allen, Penn (Pacers)
Dave Wohl, Penn (Rockets)	Ira Bowman, Penn (76ers)
Corky Calhoun, Penn (Suns)	Jim Blackwell, Dartmouth (Celtics)
Phil Hankinson, Penn (Celtics)	
Bob Bigelow, Penn (Kings)	
Tony Price, Penn (Clippers)	
Jim McMillian, Columbia (Lakers)	
Dave Newmark, Columbia (Bulls)	

The Decline

Of the 13 Golden Age players to reach the NBA, all but one (Tony Price) had matriculated to the Ivy League by 1972, thereby marking 1964-1972 as the peak period of prominence as reflected in the national rankings of that era:

Year	Peak Ranking	Year	Peak Ranking
1965	Princeton #3 (Final 4)	1973	Penn #16
1966	Penn #23	1974	
1967	Princeton #3	1975	Penn #7, PU #8(NIT)
1968	Columbia #6, PU #8	1976	Princeton #15
1969	Columbia #14	1977	
1970	Penn #13	1978	Penn #16
1971	Penn #3	1979	Penn #4 (Final 4)
1972	Penn #3, PU #14		

Furthermore, many of the 13 stars not only reached the NBA but also had long and significant careers. Most prominent were Bill Bradley, Geoff Petrie and Brian Taylor of Princeton and Jim McMillian of Columbia.

Without dwelling at length, because it is common knowledge among sports fans, amateur historians and avid New York Knicks fans; after Bradley returned from his Rhodes Scholarship hiatus at Oxford, he joined the Knicks and became a critical cog in the apparatus of the great Knick championship teams along with Walt Frazier, Willis Reed, Dave Debusschere and Dick Barnett. During his 10 year career, he was an NBA All-Star and later a member of the Hall of Fame.

6'4" Geoff Petrie, unknown to all but those who truly understand and appreciate basketball, was the best player in Ivy League history. He was a better player than Bill Bradley ... not a greater icon, role model, cult hero, scholar-athlete or legend ... just a superior basketball player. This fact became glaringly obvious once Petrie reached the NBA. After joining the Portland Trailblazers in 1970, he became the Rookie of the Year and during his injury shortened 6 year career he averaged nearly 25 PPG when healthy and scored over 50 points twice. Along with Bob McAdoo, Pete Maravich, and Kareem Abdul-Jabaar he was among the NBA's top offensive players, and the Trailblazers later retired his jersey. At Princeton, Petrie's offensive prowess was somewhat stifled by the installation of the famed Princeton offense after Pete Carril succeeded Butch van Breda Kolff in 1967. However, his NBA career enabled him to demonstrate his true ability.

Brian Taylor was a 6'2" guard who was Petrie's match as an all-around athlete and only slightly behind him as an elite basketball player. Both Petrie and Taylor were

All-State football players (Taylor's brother, Bruce, was a star defensive back for the San Francisco 49ers) in addition to being great basketball players. After Princeton, Taylor became the ABA Rookie of the Year for the New York Nets and was a star on the Nets championship teams led by Julius Erving. He was both an ABA All-Star and a member of the NBA All-Defensive team. Except for Yale's Chris Dudley and Penn's Matt Maloney, Jeremy Lin is the first significant Ivy League NBA player since Taylor retired in 1982.

If Celtic Hall of Fame center, Bill Russell, had been shorter, he would have had a game similar to that of Jim McMillian. At Columbia and later as a star forward for the championship Lakers team led by Chamberlain and West, McMillian was the ultimate winner. He won championships wherever he went and was a team player with a great all-around game. He was a scorer, a rebounder, a passer as well as a consummate leader.

The Ending

Although not at the All-Star level, John Hummer (Braves/Clippers), Corky Calhoun (Suns), Dave Wohl (Rockets) and Armond Hill (Hawks) all had productive and lengthy NBA careers. Again, except for Penn's Tony Price, 1972 was the last year that NBA-caliber recruits flocked to the Ivy League on a consistent basis. Penn's 1979 Final Four appearance, on the undercard of the

Magic Johnson - Larry Bird duel, provides for a notable and fitting end to the Golden Age. However, the demise began in Jadwin Gym on December 6, 1971 ... the day that Princeton routed North Carolina or as Don McLean sang that same year, "the day the music died." On that date the Ivy League's parity with the best national teams and conferences began to slip away, transforming the Golden Age into a "Basketball Brigadoon" ... a wistful, nostalgic and sentimental memory.

Finally, the reason that Harvard's James Brown is so integral to the Golden Age narrative is that, post-Bradley, the Ivy League had unconsciously established a premium basketball brand. It was capable of competing with North Carolina and Duke for strong academic, NBA-caliber recruits even at non-traditional basketball schools like Harvard. Brown and teammate Floyd Lewis recounted recently that they went to Harvard to win an Ivy League championship with full expectation of going on to the NBA. They understood that this could be achieved because it had been done by numerous Ivy League players between 1965 and 1970. For them and other erstwhile McDonald's All-Americans, going to the Ivy League to play basketball was not perceived as a stumbling block but rather as a stepping stone to the NBA ... to a limited extent, the way Kentucky is perceived in 2013.

Hall of Fame St. Anthony's High School coach, Bob

Hurley, has noted that the reason long-time patrician programs such as North Carolina and Duke maintain their recruiting success year in and year out is due to "the power of their brand." Similar to Procter & Gamble, they work meticulously at developing and managing their brand. They have a successful brand strategy and, as with any good business, they execute with precision ... success breeds success.

Princeton, Penn, and other Ivy League teams between 1964 and 1972 also had NBA-caliber, world-class recruiting brands. However, unlike Duke and North Carolina, there was never a conscious brand development/management strategy. Their brand excellence occurred via "spontaneous combustion." Bill Bradley was deservedly immaculated by the national press (specifically *The New York Times*) and the concomitant massive free publicity resulted in a decade of elite brand status and awareness. The coaching cum "Barnum and Bailey" genius of Butch van Breda Kolff, the excellence of Bill Bradley and the hype of *The New York Times* (GAIB = VBK + $Bill x NY Times) combined to serve as a catalyst for Ivy League basketball transcendence. However, as there never was a "conscious" brand development effort to begin with, the serendipitous Golden Age of Ivy League basketball was destined to slowly fade away into the ether of "Basketball Brigadoon." By 1979, this fading process was complete and the Golden Age was officially over ... a remote, bygone era.

Atlantic Coast Conference Versus Ivy League (1964--1972) First Round Draftees	
ACC*	**Ivy**
1) Billy Cunningham (1965) North Carolina/76ers	1) Bill Bradley (1965) Princeton/Knicks
2) Jack Marin (1966) Duke/Now Wizzards	2) Jim McMillian (1970) Columbia/Lakers
3) Charlie Scott (1970) North Carolina/Virginia Squires (ABA)	3) Geoff Petrie (1970) Princeton/Trailblazers
4) Bob McAdoo (1972) North Carolina/Now Clippers	4) John Hummer (1970) Princeton/Now Clippers
	5) Brian Taylor(1972) Princeton/Nets (ABA)
	6) Corky Calhoun (1972) Penn/Suns

* Traditional core: North Carolina, Duke, NC State, Wake Forest, Clemson, Maryland and Virginia.

1968...Tigers Versus Tar Heels

1) No. 8 ranked Princeton had two first round draftees(Geoff Petrie, John Hummer) as well as three later round draftees (Joe Heiser, John Haarlow, Chris Thomforde)...Princeton came in 2nd in the Ivy League to Columbia that year.

2) No.2 North Carolina had one first round draftee (Charlie Scott) as well as four later round draftees (Bill Bunting, Larry Miller, Dick Grubar, Rusty Clark)...

North Carolina won the ACC Championship and lost to UCLA (Lew Alcindor) in the National Championship game.

Conclusion

During the "teeth of the Golden Age" (1964—1972), the caliber of players and the level of play in the ACC and the Ivy League were strikingly similar. The final four, '68 Tar Heels arguably had "lesser talent" than the '68 Tigers who came in 2nd place in the Ivy League.

The Ivy League's "Magnificent Eleven" includes the 11 players who achieved a "significant career" in the NBA following their college tenure. In addition, Jeremy Lin is included as a 12th honorary member of this group by virtue of his truly historical (and Linsane) accomplishments during the month of February 2012, as well as his signing a $25 million three year contract with the Houston Rockets in July of the same year.

A significant NBA player is defined as follows:

1. A player who, at minimum, establishes himself as a productive role player and whose career lasts between 5-10 years.
2. In addition, a player who signs a second, more lucrative long-term NBA contract assuring a level of financial security.

As such, the Magnificent Eleven members range from Hall of Fame New York Knick icon, Bill Bradley, to solid role player and subsequent New Jersey Net head coach, Dave Wohl.

The Ivy League's significant NBA players are listed in chronological order as follows:

Rudy LaRusso/Dartmouth	Corky Calhoun/Penn
Bill Bradley/Princeton	Brian Taylor/Princeton
Jim McMillian/Columbia	Armond Hill/Princeton
Geoff Petrie/Princeton	Chris Dudley/Yale
John Hummer/Princeton	Matt Maloney/Penn
Dave Wohl/Penn	Jeremy Lin/Harvard

"Linsanity"

Why was Jeremy Lin's February eruption so unique and special? He went from a desultory existence as a soon-to-be-released bench player who was sleeping on a couch as of February 1st, to being featured on the cover of *Sports Illustrated*--two weeks in succession--as of March 1st. Given a chance to start due to injury, Lin led the Knicks--a team with an 8-15 record--on a 9-2 streak. He generated the following statistics during an 11-game stretch between February 4th and February 22, 2012:

	Points	Assists
Nets	25	7
Jazz	28	8
Wizards	23	10
Lakers	38	7
Timberwolves	20	8
Raptors	27	11
Kings	10	13
Hornets	26	5
Mavericks	28	14
Nets	21	9
Hawks	17	9
Average	23.9	9.3

His 38 point victorious duel versus Lakers superstar, Kobe Bryant, occurred under the bright lights of "the world's most famous arena", Madison Square Garden. In addition, his Harvard pedigree and Asian heritage added a global, cosmopolitan dimension to the story line, which the sports media-complex found impossible to resist. At length, Jeremy Lin was a male-Cinderella, rags-to-riches story with an Ivy League patina.

Tom Heinsohn, Rudy LaRusso, Bill Russell

Geoff Petrie, Jerry West

John Hummer and venture capital partner Ann Winblad

Yale's Chris Dudley

Larry Bird, Armond Hill and Tom McMillen

Corky Calhoun, Phil Jackson

CHAPTER 2

Princeton: "Primus Inter Pares" (1960-1969)

Princeton and Philadelphia share a remote and ironic relationship. The state of New Jersey is densely populated and most of its residents live in either greater New York City or greater Philadelphia. While Princeton and Philadelphia are extremely close to one another (only 32 miles between Northeast Philadelphia and southwestern Princeton Township as the crow flies) and many Philadelphians have historically attended Princeton University, the town of Princeton itself most definitely lies within the sphere of influence of New York City. Along with Yale and Columbia, it is one of the three Ivies that considers "the greatest city in the world" to be its hometown.

Most Philadelphians perceive Princeton as a foreign land-- a distant curiosity having no bearing whatsoever on their closed-shell-of-a-world. To a Philadelphian, Princeton is northern New Jersey and Philadelphia is all about southern New Jersey or, more precisely, "down the shore."

As Philadelphians see it, South Jersey consists of some suburbs and pine barrens that lie between them and Atlantic City, Ocean City and Cape May….also known as "Philadelphia by the sea." In their minds these New Jersey shore towns are an extension of Pennsylvania and are historically ruled by Philadelphia royalty (specifically, Grace Kelly of East Falls and Ocean City aka Princess Grace of Monaco). Northern New Jersey on the other hand is, well, "North Jersey!". It has nothing to do with anything. A Philadelphian can spend his entire life and never go to North (above Trenton) Jersey… Princeton is in North Jersey!

Conversely, a Princetonian's view of Philadelphia is similar to a Manhattanite's view of anything west of the Hudson River. To a Princetonian, Philadelphia is a large city that lies somewhere between Trenton and Los Angeles; out of sight, out of mind. Typically, a Princetonian doesn't know much about Philadelphia, and could care even less. Yet in basketball terms, Princeton University and the University of Pennsylvania share one of the great rivalries in college sports history.

Basketball notwithstanding, Princeton has a much greater affinity with its rival New York City oriented Ivies, Columbia and Yale. If one desires to attend a New York-oriented Ivy, there are three distinct options. Yale is the Connecticut Ivy…barely New England, but all New York suburbs (Greenwich, New Canaan and Darien). However, the city of New Haven itself is not the most attractive locale, more grunge than posh. While Yale University is historic and dignified, New Haven is more dull and drab.

Columbia, like Penn, is a major research university possessing a world-class complex of graduate schools. Unlike Princeton and Yale, Columbia is actually located in the "Big Apple." It is not a satellite of New York City, but rather in the heart of the city itself, Manhattan. Columbia is colossal and chaotic. It is a center of social and political controversy, and has been for decades. Unfortunately, Columbia is also the recipient of a cruel geographic practical joke.

Somehow during the past 200 years, New York University has evolved and expanded in the neighborhood that should rightfully belong to Columbia. NYU is located in Greenwich Village at the base of Fifth Avenue. It is halfway between Wall Street and midtown and right in the middle of the action. It is a vibrant and exciting location, pulsating with energy and electricity. In contrast, Columbia is located in Morningside Heights, at the far-western edge of Manhattan Island. Speaking of "out of sight, out of mind," if one had to contrive a more remote location in which to place a great world-class university--within the confines of a great world-class city-- one would be hard pressed to conjure up a more insipid outpost. At least Penn, while physically and institutionally similar to Columbia in many ways, is located in the heart of Philadelphia within walking distance of all "Center City." Columbia, on the other hand, lies on an elevated, closeted shelf in the far corner of the attic, tenuously attached to New York City.

If Yale is dignified but dull and Columbia is colossal and chaotic, then Princeton is the New York-oriented Ivy that some would suggest is pristine and perfect. There are many caricatures of the classic college town with the ideal ivy-covered campus…they are all based on Princeton University. Every other small college town in the U.S.A. aspires to be, or at least look like, Princeton. Unfortunately, Princeton's "small college town" aura has been replaced by a bustling city feel, as employment growth at both the "town" and "gown" level has resulted in significant rush hour traffic jams for those attempting to navigate its crowded streets. Princeton is a pleasure to walk but a nightmare to drive. Still, its unique setting and relatively easy access to Manhattan are very appealing to prospective commuters and students alike.

From a sporting perspective, Princeton and its fellow Ivies are central to the development of intercollegiate competition in America. Their sports tradition and heritage precedes that of more familiar modern day powers (Alabama in football or UCLA in basketball) by decades. Scholastic sports activity in the United States was inherited from established sporting tradition in England. Sport and sportsmanship became integral to British culture as early as the 18th century, and by the mid-1800s, Britain considered itself to be a "proud sporting nation." A sportsman was one who adhered to the rules of the game, practiced self-control, was indifferent to adversity and was guided by a personal code of honor which engendered fair play. In a word, sportsmanship was a distillation of ancient chivalric ideals. The 1981 film, *Chariots of Fire*, captures the extent that nerve, tenacity and skill combine to create a behavioral underpinning for a young man's character development, which could then support him throughout life's endeavors. It is this British sporting tradition first established at England's public schools and universities such as Oxford and Cambridge, that was imported by Ivy League universities in the second half of the 19th century. Over the past one hundred and fifty years, this ancient tradition has evolved into "March Madness", "The Final Four" and the "BCS Football Championship Game" as well as numerous other lucrative NCAA sports spectacles. Such are the miracles of our enlightened, modern civilization. As an advanced 21st century culture, we have somehow transformed King Arthur's chivalric "code of honor" into King James' "taking his talents to Miami"... only in America.

Princeton University itself is famous for participation in the first college football game versus Rutgers University in 1869. At that point, the university was already 123 years old and established as one of America's elite institutions.

Princeton proper consists of the university on one side of Nassau Street and the town on the other side. "Town and Gown" tradition held that the university was "primus inter pares" or 'first among equals." As the university's reputation grew and developed in the 20th century, so did the stature of Princeton as a community. By the 1920's and 1930's, sporting activity had also evolved with the institutions of Harvard, Yale, Princeton and Penn taking a leading role in the development of collegiate football as well as the Olympic sports comprising track and field competition.

By the outset of World War II, collegiate athletics consisted primarily of sports stemming from the "British tradition" (football, track, rowing, tennis, fencing, golf) as opposed to those of "American invention" (baseball and basketball). However, during and after World War II, basketball, which was invented by Dr. James Naismith in 1891, continued its rise in prominence among Ivy League universities. Curiously, both Dartmouth and Harvard were among the early high achievers of what would become Ivy League basketball during the pre-Bradley years (1940-1962).

The NCAA Tournament for crowning a national collegiate basketball champion was first held in the spring of 1939, and Villanova defeated Brown, 42-30, in the very first game. However, this was rather untimely as the world was about to enter six years of catastrophic war. At the end of the 1930's, there was only one big team sport in the United States and that was our national pastime, Major League Baseball. Everything else was secondary. The NBA would not be founded until after the war, while the NFL, which was established in the 1920's, was still more sandlot than stadium-based. During the war years from 1940 to 1945, the NCAA Tournament was able to develop the "green shoots" that would later support its decades of continuous growth. Interestingly, one of the early Final Fours (or Final Twos back then) included a pre-Ivy League Dartmouth team which was comprised of maybe the most unique combination of players in tournament history.

The 1944 Dartmouth squad, referred to as "the soldier team," consisted of players like U.S. Marine Harry Leggat, who was a former New York University star. Also on the team were Bob Gale, formerly of Cornell, and Dick McGuire, a proven St. John's star and future NBA Hall of Famer, who was assigned to Dartmouth by the Navy V-12 Program (a U.S. Marine Officer Training Program). Needless to say the recruiting process for Dartmouth's 1944 team was quite different from any that Kentucky Coach John Calipari might undertake today...still it worked. Unfortunately, despite having a team of older, talented soldiers, Dartmouth fell to the University of Utah in the championship game. In retrospect, the most salient aspect of the 1944 NCAA Tournament was that the championship game was played before a record crowd of more than 15,000 at New York's Madison Square Garden, establishing college basketball as a premiere, must-see sporting event .

After the war, one of the early stars of the NBA was Princeton's own Bud Palmer. Palmer was twenty-five by the time he joined the New York Knickerbockers in 1946. The NBA forerunner, Basketball Association of America, had just been established and the dormant period of sports activity due to the war was ending. Palmer only played three seasons for the Knicks. However, he was the Knicks' first captain and averaged nearly 13 points per game (ppg). In addition to his on court prowess, he later went on to become a leading play-by-play announcer for NBA television broadcasts during the 1950's and 1960's… the Jim Nance of the era. As such, Palmer was a true pioneer of NBA basketball as we know it today. He was also credited as one of the pioneers of the "jump shot", fundamentally changing the way the game is played.

The Ivy League was not officially established until 1956, so up until that point most schools were playing as quasi-independents. However, the first dominant team of the newly formed Ivy League was Dartmouth led by All-American power forward Rudy LaRusso. Between 1956 and 1959, Dartmouth and LaRusso rendered the Penn-Princeton rivalry stillborn by winning three championships. It was not until 1960 that Princeton teams, led by Jim Brangan and Pete Campbell, won successive championships. This set the table for the Bill Bradley era of consecutive championships between 1963 and 1965. It also set the table for the arrival of Butch van Breda Kolff, who coached the five most successful years in Princeton history. VBK also attracted more NBA-caliber recruits than any coach in Ivy League history.

Post-WW II, the town of Princeton settled into Camelot-mode. While John F. Kennedy's administration projected a Camelot illusion, Princeton's "Town and Gown" was the real deal. It was a storybook setting of high-end shops, such as Langrock Men's Clothing, that were nestled in the shadow of ivy-covered walls. Bill Bradley's arrival as an athletic and academic deity only fed the Princeton community's cosseted sense of superiority and entitlement. The prevailing mindset was that Princeton is "a cut above the rest of the world," so of course it deserves a basketball star/ Rhodes Scholar who himself is a "cut above mere mortals…" even a cut above other first team All-Americans such as Cazzie Russell and Dave Stallworth, both future New York Knicks teammates of Bradley. Russell and Stallworth did not share the sentiment.

Bradley's graduation in 1965 coincided with the onset of social unrest stemming from the Civil Rights Movement; as well as campus radicalism stemming from concerns about the Vietnam War, and the real threat of military conscription imposed by the draft. While the impact of these societal tidal waves hit campuses like Columbia and Cal- Berkley head on, Princeton remained in its ivy-covered cocoon for several more years. All the while the quality of its basketball recruiting was enhanced even further as Coach van Breda Kolff attracted high school All-Americans from the Philadelphia area, northern New Jersey and metro Washington D.C. In addition, according to legendary recruiting guru Howard Garfinkel, Princeton was one of Lew Alcindor's top three choices along with U.C.L.A. and St. John's (Dynasty anyone?). As the 1960s came to a close, Princeton had established itself as a national basketball power. The Tigers had won nine Ivy League championships, achieved three Top 10 rankings, and two Top 5 rankings in addition to its 1965 Final Four appearance…all between 1959 and 1969. Princeton was indeed "Primus Inter Pares" in terms of Ivy League basketball.

When Coach van Breda Kolff left Princeton in 1967 for the Los Angeles Lakers, he was succeeded by one of his former players, Coach Pete Carril. Upon his arrival, one might say that the "Old Mother Hubbard…the cupboard was bare" nursery rhyme was the ultimate inaccurate allegory. In fact, the cupboard was stocked with the most talented team in Princeton history. While the 1967 Princeton team achieved a No. 3 ranking, the 1968 team's talent level was superior. It consisted of future NBA All-Star Geoff Petrie, future NBA starter John Hummer and future NBA draftees Joe Heiser, John Haarlow and

Chris Thomforde. Even including the 1965 Bradley-led Final Four team, the '68 team was the greatest assemblage of basketball talent in Ivy League history, the likes of which has not been seen since. This team represented the final embodiment of Coach van Breda Kolff's recruiting genius.

However, even as the Princeton teams of both 1968 and 1969 were virtual Goliaths in terms of their NBA-caliber basketball talent, their fortunes declined after VBK left for the NBA. There was a "new kid on the block" which was determined to knock Princeton, with its smug Bradley-aura, off its proto-dynastic perch.

Columbia, one of the three New York City-oriented Ivies, not only provided Princeton's '68 team with competition, but convincingly won the Ivy League championship. How was it possible for a Princeton goliath with a future NBA All-Star, a future NBA starter and three future NBA draftees to lose intra-league? Easy...the Columbia team that they faced included Jim McMillian, the future forward of the 69-13 NBA Champion Los Angeles Lakers. These Lakers also included Wilt Chamberlain, Jerry West, Gail Goodrich, Happy Hairston and sixth man, Pat Riley. This 1972 Laker team had the longest winning streak in NBA history (33 games) and is still considered by many to be the greatest team of all-time, including Michael Jordan's Bulls. In addition to McMillian, Columbia had 7' 0" center Dave Newmark, who went on to play for the

Chicago Bulls, as well as future NBA draftees Hayward Dotson and Roger Walaszak. Finally, shoring up the front court was future Washington Redskins Super Bowl lineman, John Starke. Demonstrating Ivy League depth, the 1968 Penn team was also steeped in talent but came in a distant third place. Nationally, Columbia was ranked No. 6 while second place Princeton was ranked No. 8. Two Ivy League schools ranked in the Top 10! This was not unique as it would happen several other times during the Golden Age era.

The crucial point is that the 1968 rivalry among Princeton, Columbia and Penn was typical of the post-Bradley Golden Age; nationally-ranked powers laden with entire lineups full of NBA talent, some at the All-Star level, butting horn's in full bull ram fashion. In the late 1960's, Ivy League basketball stature was reminiscent of the ACC in 2013. This level of talent was not destined to last in the long run, but while it lasted between 1964 and 1975, the Ivy League was one of the national power conferences…a veritable Goliath.

The New York media intensively followed Princeton and Columbia, while farther south in Philadelphia, Penn and its historic Palestra hosted hometown Big Five rivals: Villanova, Temple, La Salle and St. Joseph's as well as other nationally-ranked visiting teams such as St. Bonaventure (Bob Lanier), Niagara (Calvin Murphy) and UMass (Julius Erving). Top NBA-caliber recruits of academic distinction were attracted like magnets to the palpable excitement and high level of competition to be found in Ivy League basketball.

The influence of the media during this pre-ESPN developmental period was critical to Ivy League success. During the Golden Age, New York City was then (and always will be) the media capital of the world. Both Princeton and Columbia reside within its orbit and greatly benefitted from the media spotlight. This was the "Mad Men" era of advertising and promotion, blended with the 1920's Damon Runyon-esque tendency to create larger than life heros: Jim Brown and Johnny Unitas in football, Mickey Mantle and Willie Mays in baseball, Jack Nicholas and Arnold Palmer in golf, all fit the central casting mold of sports superstardom.

The New York Knicks during the 1960's were the "doormat" of the NBA. By enrolling at Princeton, within the New York media orbit, Bill Bradley killed two birds with one stone. As possibly the greatest college basketball player in history (the only contenders up until that point in 1965 were Bill Russell, Oscar Robertson and Jerry West), not only was he the New York media's own golden child, but he also was the potential savior of a woeful New York Knicks franchise. Madison Square Garden demanded the best and by selecting Bradley in the NBA territorial draft, the Knicks would assure that the New York media spotlight would remain on him, the Knicks and MSG for another decade after his Princeton graduation. An obscure draft history footnote is that mid-town Manhattan is 44 miles from Princeton's Nassau Hall while center city Philadelphia is 45 miles away. If these mileage numbers had been reversed, Bradley would have been playing for the Philadelphia 76ers instead of the New York Knicks.

By taking his Rhodes Scholarship interlude, Bradley unwittingly delayed the commingling of "Princeton class" with "New York Knick/Walt Frazier panache," but this only added to his mystique. Ironically, this delay created an impeccably timed admixture which resulted in the great Knicks championship teams of 1970 and 1973. For the past forty years, the New York sports media and Knicks fans have been longing for this Bradley, Frazier, DeBusschere chemistry to be replicated. The recent Jeremy Lin "Linsanity" hysteria is indicative of the years of repressed frustration.

In summary, by 1968 not only had Bill Bradley and Coach Butch van Breda Kolff established Princeton as a national collegiate basketball power (dynasty?), but via the Knicks territorial draft rights of Bradley, one of the key building blocks of a two-time NBA championship team had been put on permanent display at Madison Square Garden. The New York sports media couldn't ask for anything more. As a result, the 1960's truly were the "Princeton decade" at both the NCAA and NBA level.

As the 1960's ended, Penn was in the process of becoming a consistent national power and about to begin a decade of Ivy League basketball domination. The Bradley era, New York-centric storyline was slowly shifting southward toward Philadelphia. By 1970, an Ivy League basketball landscape in which Princeton was "Primus Inter Pares" was being transformed and the classic vignette known as "The Philadelphia Story" was about to replace it.

What Is World-Class/NBA-Caliber and Why Does It Matter?

"World-class" indicates the highest level of achievement related to a specific area of endeavor..."the best and brightest". Members of the world-class category represent the cutting-edge engine of innovation, attainment and leadership. Some examples might include the following:

- **Professional Athletics** - Roster membership in the NBA, NFL, MLB, PGA, ATP, etc.
- **Olympic Participation** - The 2012 U.S. Olympic team had 600 members.
- **Entrepreneurial Success** - Private business development and expansion benefitting society at large.
- **Tenured Professorship** - At a highly regarded academic institution.

- **<u>Undergraduate Acceptance</u>** - At a USNWR* highly selective institution
- **<u>Wall Street Partnership</u>** - At a top-ranked investment bank, law firm, hedge fund, etc.
- **<u>Top 25 USA TODAY Rankings</u>** - In basketball, football, etc.
- **<u>Politics</u>** - Member of Congress (this category is an oxymoron in that the higher the level of attainment, the greater degree of derision attached to the politician).
- **<u>Fortune 500 Corporations</u>** - Pillars of economic growth and societal stability.
- **<u>Federal Judgeship</u>** - Stewards of the legal system and the rule of law.
- **<u>Elite Secondary School Acceptance</u>** - Future leaders developed at private (Andover, Mass.) and public (Stuyvesant, NYC) secondary schools.

These are just a few examples of "world-class" categories. They are punctuated by the most elite subsets of human achievement (Sports Hall of Fame, Olympic Gold Medal, Nobel Prize, MacArthur Genius Award, Corporate CEO, Private General Partner, Governor or Senator, Supreme Court Justice, the Papacy and, of course, the highest level of human achievement, the Commissioner of the NFL).

---

*   U.S. News and World Report

Connecticut

Greater New York City/Greater
Philadelphia Area

New Haven/Yale

Syracuse/Cornell
"Excellent Lacrosse"

Boston/Harvard
"Excellent Hockey"

New Canaan/Darien

Columbia
NYC

North Jersey

Pennsylvania

Princeton

Trenton

Spring Lake

London/Oxford
"Excellent Soccer"

Bay Head

Philadelphia
Penn/Inter-AC Schools

Los Angeles/
Lakers/UCLA
"Excellent Basketball"

South Jersey

Atlantic City
"Excellent Seafood"

Ocean City

Baltimore/Washing
ton D.C./DeMatha
"Excellent High
School Basketball
and Lacrosse"

Cape May

CHAPTER 3

Penn: The Philadelphia Story (1970-1979)

The foundation for Penn's 1970's domination of Ivy League basketball was established in the 1960's by Coach Jack McClosky. However, the cultural inevitability of Penn basketball distinction lay in the historic role of basketball in the "City of Brotherly Love," as well as the university's central role in basketball history.

The University of Pennsylvania was founded in 1740 by Benjamin Franklin. Its historical sports progression parallels that of the other Ivies throughout the 19th century. As with the others, the traditional British-derived sports of football, tennis, and rowing all held a prominent position within the context of Penn's sporting tradition. Penn's football program was nationally significant in the 1930's and 40's as its teams regularly hosted the likes of Notre Dame and Michigan at Franklin Field. Its 1945 game versus Army with Heisman Trophy winners Glenn Davis and Doc Blanchard was the equivalent of Alabama versus Notre Dame today. Yet, while many Ivy League universities have distinguished football pedigrees, Penn holds a special place in the historical development of two sports in particular…one of "British tradition" and the other of "American invention."

Of "British tradition," track and field at the collegiate and scholastic level begins with the Penn Relays at Franklin Field. First held in 1895, the relays are the longest running, uninterrupted track meet in the world. Initially comprised of teams from Princeton and other Ivies, the meet went international in 1920 with the inclusion of Oxford and Cambridge. Today, high school and college teams from around the world participate in the multi-day carnival. In fact, with 15,000 runners currently participating in 300 events, one could reclassify the Penn Relays as *Chariots of Fire* for the masses."

The second sport, this one of "American invention," to have a unique Penn/Philadelphia heritage is basketball. The first five man intercollegiate basketball game was played in Philadelphia on March 20, 1897 between the University of Pennsylvania and Yale University. Tantamount to Princeton's first football game versus Rutgers in 1869, this game was the initial step in a journey leading directly to the 2013 NCAA Tournament Final Four in Atlanta. Basketball, in both historical and cultural terms, is held in higher regard in Philadelphia than in any other city. The closest analogy might be the role of lacrosse in the city of Baltimore…or jazz in the city of New Orleans .

In addition to hosting the first college basketball game, Penn has the 9th winningest program and plays in one of the oldest and most revered arenas in college basketball history. The Palestra, a Greek term for gymnasium, sits adjacent to historic Franklin Field along the banks of the Schuylkill River. Unfortunately, sometime in the mid-20th century, the Schuylkill Expressway (aka the "sure kill" expressway) was constructed, thus undermining the scenic setting with both noise and congestion. The Palestra is known by various appellations and one of the most familiar is "the cathedral of college basketball." In its capacity as a cathedral, the Palestra—and to an equal extent Madison Square Garden—has served to support and nurture the development of scholastic, collegiate and professional basketball since its completion in 1927.

In the scholastic realm Penn, via both the Penn Relays at Franklin Field and basketball at the Palestra, provided critical support to the development of these two sports. This support was transmitted through Penn's mentoring relationship with the private school Interacademic League. Established in 1887, the Inter-ac consists of William Penn Charter School (Penn's prep school, founded by William Penn in 1689), Germantown Academy (America's first country day school founded in 1759), Haverford School, Episcopal Academy, Chestnut Hill Academy and Malvern Prep. Penn Charter and Germantown Academy have the nation's oldest continuous scholastic football rivalry beginning in 1887...several years earlier than that between Andover and Exeter. Given the relationship between Penn and the Inter-ac, it is not surprising that when the Penn Relays officials decided to expand their meet in the late 1890's, the Inter-ac schools were among the newly invited participants. Likewise, when the Palestra became a significant host to the developing sport of basketball in the late 1920's, Inter-ac schools were integrally involved.

During the 1930's, Penn and its Palestra continued to lead the expansion of basketball as a growing and popular sport, both locally and nationally. After World War II, the Palestra became the host to regional high school and college games and tournaments. Then in 1954, the "Big 5" was established as an unofficial "official" league; thus formalizing the rivalries that long existed among Philadelphia's five basketball powers: Penn, Villanova, Temple, St. Joseph's and La Salle.

At the high school level, the basketball tradition that initially descended from Penn to the Interacademic League schools was extended to subsume both the Philadelphia Catholic and Public Leagues, as well as the suburban Pennsylvania Interscholastic Athletic Association (State Championship Tournament). By 1960, Penn and its Palestra had transformed what was essentially "basketball virgin ground" in 1927 into the "mother lode" of basketball tradition. Philadelphia had become the "Cradle of American Basketball."

As the cornerstone institution of basketball in America, it is quite understandable that, among the Ivies, Penn placed a higher priority on fielding a superior basketball program. In the pre-Ivy League era (prior to 1956), Penn, as a member of the Eastern Intercollegiate League, won 14 championships. Penn's first NBA-caliber star was Ernie Beck, a 6' 4" Philadelphia high school phenomenon who broke all of the school's scoring and rebounding records. He averaged more than 20 PPG throughout his career and led the Quakers to the 1953 Sweet 16. He also was a key player on the 1956 Philadelphia Warriors NBA championship team which featured Paul Arizin and Tom Gola.

During the early years of the Ivy League from 1956 through Bill Bradley's senior year in 1965, first Dartmouth and then Princeton were the dominant teams. Penn finally broke through, winning the 1966 Ivy League championship under legendary Coach Jack McClosky. Princeton, led by Geoff Petrie and John Hummer, and Columbia, led by Jim McMillian and Dave Newmark, fielded NBA-laden, nationally-ranked teams in the late 1960's. However, under the tutelage of Coach Dick Harter, who had succeeded McClosky in 1967, the Quakers were about to reap the harvest of three years of NBA-caliber recruiting.

By 1970, high school All-Americans Steve Bilsky, Dave Wohl and Jim Wolf were seasoned juniors at Penn.

They were then joined by sophomores Corky Calhoun and Bobby Morse creating a formidable combination which resulted in a second Penn Ivy League championship as well as a No.13 national ranking. Talent-wise, 1970 was also the strongest overall year in Ivy League history as Penn and Princeton with two top round NBA draft selections each (Calhoun, Wohl, Petrie and Hummer) and Columbia with one (McMillian) battled fiercely for league domination. As discussed in earlier chapters, these five players all had significant NBA careers and many of their teammates were also NBA draftees.

In the following year, 1971, the entire Penn starting team returned and was joined by a third future NBA player, Phil Hankinson. This Goliath of a team, the best in Ivy League history, was undefeated during the regular season and reached the Elite 8 before losing to Big 5 rival Villanova, a team it had defeated earlier that year at the Palestra. Penn achieved a national ranking of No. 3 in '71, but the ultimate indication of the apex of the post-Bradley Golden Age was demonstrated by a post-season coaching change.

Dick Harter, who added to Jack McClosky's success by turning Penn into a national power, decided to take the head coaching job at the University of Oregon. Penn needed a new coach and would attract one of the best in both college and NBA history. Disregard multiple NBA first round draft choices or Top 5 national rankings as indicators of a "power conference." If you want to know which leagues are dominant, look at the coaching changes. In this era, elite coaches went to the NBA and their positions were filled by coaches who wanted plum jobs at prestigious power conferences. So it was not surprising then that future Hall of Fame Coach, Chuck Daly, would leap at the opportunity to leave Boston College (now in the ACC) and pursue an "upgrade" to coach in the Ivy League - repeat - an upgrade to coach in the Ivy League. ESPN's Dick Vitale might faint! A coaching opening at Penn in 1971 would have been tantamount to a coaching opening at Kansas in 2013. From a coach's perspective, this was empirical evidence of the exceptional nature of the post-Bradley, 1964-1979, Golden Age as well as the power of the Ivy League basketball brand.

In 2013, the reservoir of Ivy League coaching expertise is deep. Today's Ivy League coaches include Harvard's Tommy Amaker, who formerly coached at Michigan, Penn's Jerome Allen, a former NBA player and Penn star, as well as Princeton's Mitch Henderson, star of the Tiger's 1998 Top 10 team. These coaches appear to be in the process of reintroducing some semblance of the "swagger" that existed back in the Golden Age…old rivalries are heating up again and new ones are developing.

Under Coach Daly, Penn's dominance continued throughout the 1970's. Penn won the Ivy League championship every year except for 1976 and 1977. It reached the Elite 8 in 1971and 1972, the Sweet 16 in 1973, and the Final Four in 1979. In between, Penn battled Princeton for league domination and usually won. However, Princeton also had its share of NBA-laden, nationally-ranked teams.

By 1972, Princeton Coach Pete Carril had fully installed what would later be coined the "famed Princeton offense." While Princeton under Coach van Breda Kolff dominated the 1960's, it was now Princeton's turn to counter-attack Coach Daly and Penn.

As previously discussed, after 1972 the post-Bradley Golden Age was in the process of slow decline. Teams with multiple NBA players and draftees—1968, '69, '70 Princeton…1968, '69 Columbia…1970, '71, '72 Penn—were being depleted through graduation. Their replacements as the decade unfolded, while talented, were with a few notable exceptions not NBA-caliber. Among the exceptions was Penn's Phil Hankinson, whose career with the Boston Celtics was cut short by injury. Also, Penn's Bob Bigelow and Princeton's Ted Manakas, both of whom played for the now Sacramento Kings. Then there were two "notable exceptions"; Brian Taylor and Armond Hill, both of whom were star guards for Princeton's nationally-ranked teams in 1972, '75 and '76, respectively.

Brian Taylor was a superior athlete who was a top draft choice of both the Seattle Sonics in the NBA and the New York Nets in the ABA. As such, he was one of the catalysts leading to the NBA/ABA merger in 1976. It may be an exaggeration to call Taylor the "Joe Namath" of professional basketball, but in some respects he was. Inter-league poaching had been going on for several years as Hall of Fame players such as Rick Barry, Julius Erving and Billy Cunningham had become subjects of free agent bidding wars. Moreover, by 1972, the bidding had entered the college ranks leading to an escalation of signing bonuses and long-term contracts. Just as had occurred between the NFL and AFL during the 1960s, it was only a matter of time until an NBA/ABA merger became the better part of valor, at least in economic terms.

Taylor was the fifth best player in Ivy League history as defined on a "body of work" (BOW) basis. A body of work analysis will be discussed in much greater detail later but, suffice it to say, it includes more than just a player's college resume. On a BOW rating scale, the five best players in Ivy history are Geoff Petrie, Bill Bradley, Rudy LaRusso, Jim McMillian, and Brian Taylor. Of course, Bill Bradley is the "greatest" player in Ivy League history and among a handful of "greatest" players in college basketball history. But he wasn't necessarily the "best" player in Ivy League history... this distinction will be explained presently.

ESPN recently conducted an impressive and comprehensive study to rank the "greatest" 25 college players of all-time. The list is as follows:

1) Lew Alcindor, UCLA
2) Oscar Robertson, Cincinnati
3) Bill Walton, UCLA
4) Bill Russell, San Francisco
5) Pete Maravich, LSU
6) Jerry West, West Virginia
7) Bill Bradley, Princeton
8) David Thompson, North Carolina State
9) Larry Bird, Indiana State
10) Wilt Chamberlain, Kansas
11) Jerry Lucas, Ohio State
12) Christian Laettner, Duke
13) Michael Jordan, North Carolina
14) Elvin Hayes, Houston
15) Magic Johnson, Michigan State
16) Patrick Ewing, Georgetown
17) Tom Gola, La Salle
18) Ralph Sampson, Virginia
19) Elgin Baylor, Seattle
20) Bob Kurland, Oklahoma State
21) Tim Duncan, Wake Forest
22) Austin Carr, Notre Dame
23) Calvin Murphy, Niagara
24) David Robinson, Navy
25) George Mikan, DePaul

Careful scrutiny of this list hints at the distinction

between the "greatest" and the "best." While Michael Jordan may be ranked the 13th "greatest" player in college basketball history (probably a correct assessment), this ranking does not preclude the fact that he is also the "best" player in all of basketball history–even though I personally prefer Kareem Abdul-Jabaar.

Taylor and Ted Manakas were the stars of Coach Carril's 1972 team, which achieved one of the most memorable victories in Ivy League history by routing Final Four-bound North Carolina and its superstar, Bob McAdoo. However, on that day future NBA draftee, center Andy Rimol, became the star of the game by rising to the occasion to outplay McAdoo and lead the Tigers with 23 points. Also on the '72 Princeton team, which attained a No.14 national ranking, were future NBA draftee Reggie Bird, Philadelphia high school legend, Jimmy Sullivan, and All-State New Jersey sharpshooter, John Berger. Again, the power and prestige of the Ivies were on display by virtue of the fact that a Princeton team, with two future NBA players and two future NBA draftees, could easily defeat a Final Four ACC champion (North Carolina), yet could not even win the Ivy League title. This confirmed the fact that as late as 1972, Penn and Princeton remained college basketball goliaths.

From 1970 to 1975, Penn won six straight Ivy League championships. Between 1973 and 1975, Penn was led at various times by NBA-bound forwards, 6'8" Phil

Hankinson and 6'9" Bob Bigelow. In addition, Big 5 Hall of Fame swing man, Ron Haigler, provided scoring firepower averaging nearly 20 ppg. Two classically groomed Philadelphia guards, savvy Ed Enoch and steady Ed Stefanski, provided direction and leadership. Enoch had been a high school star at Inter-ac League power, Penn Charter, while Stefanski had been a Philadelphia All-Catholic League performer. These Penn goliaths achieved national rankings of No.16 in 1973 and No.7 in 1975.

University of Pennsylvania teams had epic battles with Princeton powers during the mid-70s. In 1975 and '76, Princeton was led by future NBA star, Armond Hill. Also on these teams were future NBA draftees Barnes Hauptfuhrer (a Penn Charter teammate of Penn's Enoch during high school), Frank Sowinski and Tim van Blommesteyn. In addition, New York Catholic League guards Mickey Steuerer and Peter Molloy were key contributors on Princeton's 1975 NIT Championship team. Princeton teams were ranked No. 8 in 1975 and No. 15 in 1976, maintaining goliath stature.

Hill, a 6'4" point guard, was a New York Catholic League All-American who played his senior year at Lawrenceville, Princeton's prep school. A superb court general, he could be described as a shorter Magic Johnson without the "French pastry"—a technical term for Los Angeles Laker "showtime" ostentation. After Princeton, he played eight solid years in the NBA and later became the coach at Columbia University. He is currently an assistant coach for the Boston Celtics. Arriving at Princeton in 1972, he was among the last of the McDonald's level All-American recruits of the Golden Age era. As such, he successfully led Princeton's mid-decade rear guard action to keep Penn from "running the table" –winning the Ivy League championship every year of the 1970s.

The basketball pedigree of Princeton's 6'7" forward, Barnes Hauptfuhrer, contains an element of Ivy League history as well as a connection to the Penn-influenced Interacademic League. Barnes's father, George, was a star on a very good Harvard team in the pre-Ivy 1940s. He was also drafted by the Boston Celtics in 1948. Not only was he drafted by the Celtics, but he was selected No. 3 overall behind Hall of Fame stars George Mikan and Dolph Schayes. A promising NBA career appeared probable, but given the less than overwhelming economics of professional basketball at the time, he chose to enroll at the University of Pennsylvania Law School and eventually became the chairman of the venerable Philadelphia law firm, Dechert, Price and Rhodes. Therefore, in a display of Bradley-esque values one generation removed, one might say that George Hauptfuhrer sacrificed his chance for NBA stardom in order to become the classic "Philadelphia lawyer".

Given his background, 6'7" height and skill-set, Barnes helped to lead Penn Charter School to a No.1

ranking among Philadelphia area high schools in 1972. Enrolling at Princeton, which was closer to home and had a superior basketball program to Harvard at the time, he became one of the best players in school history. He also became an NBA draftee like his father.

Philadelphia's distinguished basketball heritage also extended to the NBA. The history of Villanova's Paul Arizin, La Salle's Tom Gola and, of course, Wilt Chamberlain as the leader of the great Philadelphia 76er's 1967 NBA championship team, is well established. A lesser known "Philadelphia Story" is one related to the development of the 76ers 1983 championship team. In 1973, the 76ers generated the worst record in NBA history, 9-73. In subsequent years, almost as a matter of civic duty and cultural pride, one of Philadelphia's leading citizens ascended to address the issue. Episcopal Academy Athletic Director, railroad heir and Harvard grad, Fitz Eugene Dixon bought the Philadelphia 76ers in 1976. Dixon, one of the original Forbes 400 members, proceeded to work with team management to persuade Julius Erving to join the 76ers after the completion of the ABA/NBA merger. This laid the groundwork for the later acquisition of Moses Malone and Bobby Jones, leading directly to the success of the 1983 championship team. Fitz Dixon, also a leading local philanthropist, symbolized the cities' historical commitment to, and love of, basketball as a cultural artifact. To Philadelphians at all levels, basketball is more than a game…it is a way of life.

Thacher Longstreth, a graduate of Haverford School and Princeton, Class of '41, was a close friend and associate of Fitz Dixon. He was also one of Philadelphia's most prominent civic leaders. As the head of City Council, he ran for mayor multiple times, usually losing to his archnemesis, Police Commissioner Frank Rizzo. The one thing that the "bow tie" wearing Longstreth and "billy club" wielding Rizzo agreed upon was Ivy League and Big 5 basketball which revolved around Penn and the Palestra. At 6'5", 240 pounds, Longstreth was a football legend at Princeton before World War II and was drafted by the now St. Louis Rams in 1941. He sat at midfield for every Princeton football home game for over 50 years. He also attended nearly every Penn-Princeton basketball game played at the Palestra during the Golden Age.

By 1979, the Golden Age was well into its sunset years. Coach Chuck Daly had departed Penn for the NBA but he also left behind one final gift for the university's basketball program. Between 1978 and 1983, Penn would win five straight Ivy League championships, so it was apparent that intra-league competition had diminished. However, Coach Daly's last recruiting class had "bigger fish to fry." Their number one agenda item was no longer just to beat Princeton and win another Ivy League title. By 1979, their goal was to scale basketball's Mount Everest and accomplish something that no Ivy team had achieved since Princeton and Bill Bradley in 1965. That was to reach the NCAA Final Four and, who knows, maybe even win a national championship.

The 1979 Penn squad was led by future NBA player, Tony Price, as well as NBA draftees James Salters, Matt White and Bobby Willis. Price was another in a long line of blue-chip New York City players lured to Penn. During the 1960's, elite New York prospects such as Jim McMillian and Hayward Dotson remained at home to play for Columbia. However, during the 1970's, many New Yorkers such as Hankinson, Haigler, and Price were induced to come to Philadelphia and play for Penn. As the 1979 NCAA Tournament progressed, Coach Bob Weinhauer's team advanced beating formidable foes including North Carolina (that team again!) and Syracuse. Then it won its Elite 8 matchup versus St. John's for the opportunity to play Michigan State and Magic Johnson. Penn had reached the Final Four but the national championship would have to wait. Despite being crushed 101-67, Penn unwittingly insinuated itself into a historic daily double. First, it became the second and probably last Ivy League team to reach the Final Four pinnacle. Second, Penn found itself dancing at the most celebrated Final Four spectacle in history—the beginning of the decades long rivalry and friendship between Magic Johnson and Larry Bird. The mystique of their connection is so significant and notable that in April 2012 a biographical play, "Magic/Bird," opened on Broadway.

The Golden Age had ended. Tony Price was drafted and played for the now Los Angeles Clippers before becoming a Wall Street insurance executive. For good measure, he also became the father of UConn star and current NBA player A.J. Price. His graduation marked the passing of the era of Ivy League NBA-caliber recruiting on a consistent basis. The Wilderness Years had begun. Great basketball would continue to be played, albeit with a slightly lesser talent pool. The Penn/Princeton rivalry would become even more intense, if that is possible. Princeton would devolve from being a basketball dynasty to a basketball David, the Goliath slayer. Behind the mesmerizing tedium and confusion of the "famed" Princeton offense, the Tigers would be capable, on a given day, of defeating a No. 1 ranked opponent, be it Georgetown or UCLA. The heritage of Penn and Princeton basketball would continue to grow. Still the memory of the bygone era, when Penn/Princeton matchups evoked the excitement of current Yankees/Red Sox games, will remain a fond one for those who witnessed them back in the day.

Finally, a gauge or benchmark for determining a great college team is the number of future NBA players on the roster. Similarly, the benchmark for great NBA teams is the number of future Hall of Fame players on the roster (i.e., 1973 Knicks = 6, 1986 Celtics = 5, 2013 Miami Heat = 3?). The 1985 Villanova upset of Georgetown for the NCAA title is considered by many to be the greatest tournament upset of all-time. However, this Ed Pinckney-led team included 3 future NBA players, the same number as the Patrick Ewing-led Georgetown Hoyas. Therefore, in retrospect, this historic upset was "mild" at best. The 1971 Penn Quakers had 3 future NBA players on the roster (Wohl, Calhoun and Hankinson), certainly adequate to compete for the National Chamionship against UCLA that year, which carried 4 future NBA players on its roster. ESPN analyst, Coach Dan Dakich, has often explained that in order to get to the Final Four, a team needs "three pros" (future NBA players). The 1971 Quakers definitely fulfilled this requirement. The fact that, in the 1971 Final, UCLA survived a 68-62, hard-fought battle against Villanova--a team that Penn had earlier defeated--is testament that Penn could have won the National Championship that year.

Tale of Two Cities		
Princeton **"Town and Gown"**	**Facts and Figures**	**Philadelphia** **"Penn: The Hub of Center City"**
Approximately 20,000	1970 Population	Approximately 2 Million
John Witherspoon… signer of Declaration of Independence, first president of university and ancestor of Reese Witherspoon.	Founding Fathers	William Penn… city of Philadelphia and Penn Charter School; Ben Franklin… University of Pennsylvania.
Pristine, pastoral, prestigious college town.	Setting	Ancient, historic city…populated by Main Line lawyers and rabid Eagles fans who relish throwing snowballs at Santa Claus.
Few…liberal arts and "liberal" politics.	Graduate Schools	Numerous…world-class including law, medicine, Wharton Business and Annenberg Communication.
A real life Camelot… or at least a reality show version of Camelot.	Town/City reminds one of	What New York City would be like if it didn't include Manhattan.
Dartmouth but civilized.	Ivy most similar to	Columbia but capitalist.

Tale of Two Cities		
Princeton **"Town and Gown"**	**Facts and** **Figures**	**Philadelphia** **"Penn: The Hub of** **Center City"**
Fierce rivalry…as one of the ancient "Big 3," sports rivalry dates back to jousting.	Attitude toward Harvard and Yale	Harvard and who?
Ivy most renowned for southern heritage and pretensions.	Geography	Southernmost Ivy.
Justices Sam Alito '72, Elena Kagan '79 and Sonia Sotomayor '76. Shouldn't Princetonians hold all nine seats?	Most influential living graduates	Brian Roberts '81… CEO Comcast and enthusiastic Penn basketball fan; Dave Montgomery, Penn-Wharton '70…Co-owner/ CEO Philadelphia Phillies. Other than the Papacy, sports franchise owner-ship is highest possible calling.
Lisa Halaby '73…Queen Noor of Jordan and Princeton basketball fan.	Royal personage	Grace Kelly… Princess Grace of Monaco…brother John B. Kelly III was a Penn and Olympic gold medal rower.
"Dollar Bill"	All-time sports icon	"Concrete Charlie"
Nassau Hall and Langrock's	Most famous landmarks	The Palestra and Franklin Field

CHAPTER 4

The Ivy League's Best Coaches ... Best Teams ... Best Players

In brand development and recruiting terms, a picture is worth a thousand words. There have been many iconic pictures taken throughout history: the Times Square kiss on VJ Day, the flag raising on Iwo Jima, little John Kennedy saluting his father's casket. From a basketball brand building and recruiting standpoint, the cover of *Sports Illustrated* on February 27, 1967 is as priceless as any picture taken during the 1960s. Captioned "Princeton Builds a Basketball Dynasty," it featured stars Gary Walters and Chris Thomforde, fresh from a victory over No. 2 ranked North Carolina (back in the Golden Age the Ivies beat the Tar Heels consistently).

The subsequent No. 3 A.P. ranking, coupled with the absence of Bill Bradley, apparently convinced the S.I. reporting staff that elite basketball excellence had become a permanent condition at Princeton. After all, two years earlier Princeton had reached the Final Four and a No. 3 ranking during Bill Bradley's senior year. Here it was two years later and, even without Bradley, Coach van Breda Kolff's team was still ranked No. 3. The implication was that Coach van Breda Kolff and his Tigers were destined, in *Groundhog Day* fashion, to endlessly replicate the successful formula of the previous five years and consistently achieve Top 5 rankings well into the future. One problem with this thesis was that within six months of the articles release, Coach van Breda Kolff would be gone. Willem "Butch" van Breda Kolff was a one of a kind, high energy personality who loved to compete. He actually arrived at Princeton after Bradley, but he realized that he had caught "lightening in a bottle" and immediately sold the opportunity to play with Bradley as a way to upgrade his supporting cast. Come to Princeton and be like Bill! Within three years, he had amassed an arsenal of high school All-American talent that would mature into a veritable parade of college stars and future NBA draftees. Ed Hummer, Gary Walters, Robbie Brown, Joe Heiser, John Haarlow, Chris Thomforde, Geoff Petrie, John Hummer—all would become minor legends (Bradley was the only major legend) at Princeton. Had the van Breda Kolff recruiting trend and wide-open NBA style of play continued for another ten years, maybe the S.I. dynasty prediction would have come to pass. Then again, if Lew Alcindor had decided to enroll at Princeton (a serious consideration) instead of UCLA, a dynasty may have come to pass. Regardless, neither one happened and the dynasty dreams dissipated with van Breda Kolff's departure.

Dynasty?

The following season van Breda Kolff was coaching the Los Angeles Lakers and Wilt Chamberlain. If Lew Alcindor is not available, why not "Wilt the Stilt"? In any event, the quality of players left behind for new coach, Pete Carril, was an embarrassment of riches. In addition, the prospect of continuity was reasonably high as van Breda Kolff had coached Pete Carril at Lafayette College, and Carril had coached Gary Walters in high school. This was a real life scenario of what goes around comes around. Princeton was in good hands with Coach Carril.

Yes, definitely good hands, but also different hands. In terms of playing style and personality, van Breda Kolff and Carril were quite a contrast. While van Breda Kolff's approach could be described as volatile and aggressive, letting the talent flow; Carril's approach could be described as intense and mechanical, urging the talent to mesh. Van Breda Kolff might be inclined to recruit the blue chip thoroughbreds and let them run; whereas, Carril might be inclined to recruit the right components and make them hum... specifically within the context of the precision-stoked Princeton offense which is based on: ball movement, crisp passing, back door cuts, full use of the 35-second clock, and efficient outside/three point shooting. If executed in a disciplined fashion as instructed by Coach Carril, it could be deadly effective, especially in terms of leveling the playing field versus less disciplined teams with superior athletic ability.

Van Breda Kolff was an admitted "vagabond coach" who left many jobs (especially Princeton) at the height of success. He even ended up coaching high school at age 61 after earlier in his career coaching the likes of Bill Bradley, Wilt Chamberlain, and Jerry West. Carril on the other hand was the "anti-vagabond." He coached at Princeton from 1967 to 1996. After he retired in 1996, the Tigers continued to be coached by a series of his former players and assistants including Bill Carmody, John Thompson III, Joe Scott, Sydney Johnson, and Mitch Henderson. The two tendencies that van Breda Kolff and Carril shared were their fiery sideline demeanor and their commitment to hard-nosed defense. In describing the difference between the two men, longtime acquaintance and Princeton resident, Harry Hamilton (Chip) Hall III (Yale '74), stated with elegant simplicity: " van Breda Kolff was imposing, intimidating and feared, while Carril was imposing, intimidating but beloved".

Van Breda Kolff's record at Princeton was unassailable: a 103-31 won-loss record with four Ivy championships in five years, a Final Four appearance, two Top 5 rankings, and an astounding recruiting legacy of NBA-caliber talent which will never be replicated. One could be forgiven for suggesting that the Golden Age began to die the day van Breda Kolff left for the Lakers. Although there might be some truth to this statement, it is still far too premature. While van Breda Kolff, with

"Dollar Bill" as his temporal guide, was the "Godfather of the Golden Age," enough strong underpinnings had been lain to sustain the Golden Age for another 12 years. First and foremost, the elite basketball brand had already been established, albeit unwittingly. The *New York Times/Bradley* era hype coupled with the *Sports Illustrated* talk of dynasty had solidified the image of Ivy League basketball as a path not only to national collegiate prominence but also a possible NBA career. Second, the players were in place. The 1968 Princeton team inherited by Coach Carril was the "most talented" Ivy League team of all time (though not the best). Third, Penn, Columbia, and even Harvard and Dartmouth were just beginning their challenge to Princeton's 1960s sovereignty with NBA-caliber recruits of their own. As the decade of the '60s was ending, Columbia, led by Jack Rohan and future Lakers' star, Jim McMillian, would shatter any Princeton dreams of dynasty. Meanwhile, Penn, under the leadership of Dick Harter, was stocking up for a decade of basketball dominance in the 1970s that would even surpass what Princeton had achieved in the 1960s.

All the while Princeton, under Coach Carril, was undergoing a post- van Breda Kolff transmogrification. The Carril era would cover the final 12 years of the Golden Age (1967-1979) as well as the first half of the Penn-Princeton hegemonic Wilderness Years (1980-1996). For a period of time, the consistent flow of McDonald's level All-American, NBA-caliber talent would continue, highlighted by Brian Taylor and Armond Hill. However, over the years, Princeton would become more famous for the "famed" Princeton offense than the talented players who executed it. In the late 1960s, Princeton was revered for its nationally-ranked potential dynasty as well as the All-Americans who played there. During the Wilderness Years, Princeton became revered for the ability to "pull an upset" on the nationally-ranked teams that it played (Georgetown, UCLA, etc.). It went from 1968 "Goliath" in Dick Vitale speak, to 1996 "David," the Goliath Killer.

The irony was that as the Princeton program transformed from giant to giant killer, its reputation was enhanced in the eyes of the post-ESPN national media. It seems that Princeton or Penn being the equal of North Carolina, Duke, or Indiana was not a narrative that the cable TV media was comfortable driving. After Penn's 1979 attainment/disappointment, the overwhelming non-Ivy-centric press subliminally communicated that the Ivy League should be "put back in its box" and not insinuate itself into the NCAA's premier basketball events such as the Final Four. However, the narrative of the "David vs. Goliath" upset possibility would be ideal, especially if Penn or Princeton would conveniently lose at the last minute and not disrupt the bracketology. In the post-ESPN era (1979-Present), two of Dick Vitale's primary themes became: "Duke is Great!" (Brand enhancing for

Duke in terms of attracting McDonald's All-Americans); and "Princeton is David" (Brand diminishing in terms of attracting McDonald's All-Americans).

Nonetheless, Princeton, Penn, and the other Ivies had many talented players during the post-ESPN era, including eight NBA players and 14 NBA draftees. However, the consistent drumbeat of "Princeton is David" by ESPN and others conveyed the message to potential Geoff Petries and Brian Taylors that Duke or North Carolina would be their optimal destination, not the small ball of the Ivy League.

Between 1980 and 2010, Princeton had numerous stars in addition to future New Jersey Net, Steve Goodrich. Two time Ivy League Player of the Year, Craig Robinson (brother of First Lady Michelle Obama) highlighted a series of Princeton players drafted by the NBA. These include: Bob Roma, Rich Simkus, Bill Ryan, and Kevin Mullin. While a perennial "David" at the national level, Princeton along with arch-rival Penn, remained the unquestioned power within the Ivy League. Still, the cruel irony as it relates to Butch van Breda Kolff remains to this day. The coach who led Princeton to greatness and near dynasty stature is an all but forgotten figure, possibly due to his impatient vagabond nature. Conversely, the heritage and system that transformed the Tigers from "Goliath" to "David" remains revered among so-called basketball cognoscenti, many of whom probably couldn't spell "van Breda Kolff" if put to the test. Even in 2013, the Los Angeles Lakers attempted to install the Princeton offense before Kobe Bryant mutinied and Coach Mike Brown was fired.

The loss of Ivy League elite brand status occurred over the years between the 1968 Geoff Petrie-led "Goliath" and the 1996 UCLA conquering "David." The impact of this brand loss was never more apparent than in the recruiting experience of Steve Goodrich's high school league, Philadelphia's Inter-ac. As previously discussed, the Inter-ac is an Ivy Prep League, which is a natural feeder system to the Ivy universities. Consisting of six schools: Penn Charter, Germantown Academy, Episcopal Academy, Haverford School, Chestnut Hill Academy, and Malvern Prep; the league is academically elite as well as rich in basketball tradition. With a combined male student body of only 400, the Inter-ac has placed eight players in the NBA during the past 15 years, while the Ivy League with 12 times the male enrollment has placed four. Among those eight Inter-ac players, two attended Ivies (Goodrich—Penn Charter, Princeton, Nets; and Jerome Allen—Episcopal, Penn, Pacers). Six did not (Wayne Ellington—Episcopal, North Carolina, Timberwolves; Gerald Henderson—Episcopal, Duke, Bobcats; Alvin Williams—Germantown, Villanova, Raptors; Matt Walsh—Germantown, Florida, Nets; Sean Singletary—Penn Charter, Virginia, Suns; Bob Kurz—Penn Charter, Notre Dame, Golden State).

There is a high probability that back in 1968 all eight of these NBA-caliber recruits would have attended Ivy League schools, or at the least given them very serious consideration. In addition, NBA-caliber high school All-Americans from powerful New York, Philadelphia, and Washington D.C. Catholic and Public League schools (i.e., James Brown, DeMatha; Armond Hill, Bishop Ford; Jim McMillian, Thomas Jefferson) have not recently considered the Ivies as intently as they did back in the Golden Age. Of course, academic selectivity plays a role in who attends an Ivy university (i.e., can the NBA-caliber recruits be admitted and handle the academic demands). While this is a crucial consideration, the notion that the Ivies are significant academic superiors to Stanford, Northwestern, Vanderbilt, Duke, Michigan, etc. is self-imposed, self-limiting, and self-delusional. Just refer to the U.S. News and World Report Rankings. (See post-chapter analysis).

Among Penn and Princeton's Golden Age rivals, Columbia was under the tutelage of its greatest basketball figure in history. Jack Rohan was a member of Columbia's undefeated 1951 pre-Ivy basketball team. Years later he was selected as the National Coach of the Year for leading Columbia's 1968 team to a No. 6 ranking and Sweet 16 appearance. Columbia's '68 and '69 teams, both nationally-ranked, were among the best in Ivy League history, featuring Jim McMillian, Dave Newmark, Hayward Dotson, Roger Walaszak and George Starke.

In order to underscore how strong (literally) the Columbia frontcourt of the era was, it not only featured perennial NBA star , 6'6" Jim McMillian, at small forward as well as future Chicago Bulls center, 7'0" Dave Newmark; but its most formidable member was 6'5" power forward George Starke. Like McMillian and Newmark, Starke also played professionally...but in the NFL, not the NBA! After graduation he embarked on a long and illustrious career as an offensive lineman for the Washington Redskins, and his 14 year career was crowned with a 1982 victory over the Miami Dolphins in the Super Bowl .

Princeton's Coach Carril admiringly and humorously recounted that there were only a few times when he was outsmarted by his rival coach, and each of those times Jack Rohan was the rival coach. Rohan retired from basketball in 1974 to become a tenured professor at Columbia, but he returned in 1991 to help resuscitate a dormant basketball program. He led the Lions to a second place finish in 1992 before retiring for good in 1995, at which time he was succeeded by Princeton Golden Age great, Armond Hill.

Among coaching legends at Penn... where to begin? As previously elucidated, Penn's basketball heritage extends back to 1897 and by 1956 when the Ivy League was established, the university already had a storied history. Coach Jack McClosky was a former Penn and NBA player (Philadelphia Warriors) who coached Penn between 1956 and 1966. While his teams only won the Ivy League championship once, in 1966, he laid the foundation for a series of Hall of Fame stature coaches both at the collegiate and NBA level. After his career at Penn, McClosky went to the NBA and coached the Portland Trailblazers before becoming the general manager of the Detroit Pistons. Known as "Trader Jack," he set in motion a series of trades and draft selections that ultimately led to the Pistons winning back-to-back NBA championships in 1989 and 1990. With Hall of Fame guard Isiah Thomas as the team's cornerstone, McClosky and fellow Penn great, Chuck Daly, surrounded him with the likes of Joe Dumars, Bill Laimbeer, Dennis Rodman, and Rick Mahorn... the rest is NBA history.

Dick Harter only coached at Penn for five years, 1966 to 1971, but he was the most successful coach in school history. He was also a superlative recruiter, ably assisted by his protégée, Richard "Digger" Phelps. Harter's teams were not only the best in Penn's history, but also among the best in Ivy League history, particularly the 1971 Quakers, which were 28-1 and ranked No. 3 nationally. This team was so good that when it lost to Villanova in the Elite 8, a team it had earlier defeated, the season was considered an abject failure. This assessment stemmed from the fact that Harter considered his Penn team to be superior to UCLA, led that year by Sydney Wicks and Curtis Rowe, and fully capable of winning the National Championship.

Harter coached during the height of the Golden Age and his teams were ranked No. 13 in 1970, No. 3 in 1971, No. 3 in 1972, and No. 16 in 1973. While Chuck Daly actually coached in 1972 and 1973, Penn's records and national ranking stemmed significantly from the impact of Dick Harter's NBA-caliber recruits. After a sojourn to coach at the University of Oregon, Harter later joined the Pistons and his former Penn colleagues, McClosky and Daly, before eventually becoming the head coach of the NBA expansion Charlotte Hornets.

When Chuck Daly took the reins of Penn's nationally-ranked Goliath, similar to Pete Carril's situation in replacing van Breda Kolff in 1967, the "cupboard was full" in terms of talent and potential. The 1972 Quakers were comprised of Corky Calhoun, Bobby Morse, Phil Hankinson, and Craig Littlepage, among others. Again as an indicator of overall Ivy League strength, this team handily subdued a powerful Princeton team—one that had routed Bob McAdoo-led North Carolina—on its way to another Ivy League championship and No. 3 ranking. Ditto Penn's 1973 team… Ivy League championship, No. 16 ranking. In 1973, only the faces had changed as Bob Bigelow and Ron Haigler replaced Calhoun and Morse.

Coach Daly's remaining tenure (1974-1978) evolved into a "death struggle" with his Princeton rival. Between 1974 and 1978 both schools fielded powerful teams and battled to a virtual standoff. However, in the Ivy tradition of "cupboards left brimming," Coach Daly would leave behind a talented collection of recruits for his successor, Coach Bob Weinhauer. Daly was off to an eventual Hall of Fame NBA career with the Pistons, but he would miss out on the Final Four success achieved by a nucleus of Tony Price, James Salters, Matt White, Bobby Willis and Tim Smith.

The Golden Age was ending. The 1979 Penn team may not have been as talented as some earlier Penn teams, but its heart was unsurpassed. James Salters once confided that it took several years to recover from the crushing loss to Magic Johnson and Michigan State. However, Penn's Final Four appearance was a glorious achievement for Ivy League basketball. As Larry Bird would be the first man to tell anyone who would listen, there is no disgrace in losing to Magic Johnson.

Two other Penn coaches of note are important to mention. One had a fleeting career at Penn while the other stands at the crossroads of Ivy League/Big 5 history. Digger Phelps was an assistant to Dick Harter in the late 1960s. As many sports fans are aware, Coach Phelps is a current ESPN analyst and, along with the irrepressible Dick Vitale, a leading icon of college basketball commentary. However, many television viewers today might not recall what an accomplished coach he was back in the day. First he became famous for "beating the unbeatable." This time, instead of DeMatha High School defeating

Lew Alcindor's Power Memorial team, it was Notre Dame defeating Bill Walton's UCLA team and ending its 88-game winning streak in 1974. Coach Phelps went on to lead Notre Dame to great success including a Final Four appearance in 1978. However, his truly remarkable coaching accomplishment came in the early 1970s, soon after leaving Penn. His first head coaching job was at Fordham University, which was not considered a basketball heavyweight. Yet, in his second season he coached Fordham, with future NBA starter Ken Charles, to a 26-3 record and a spot in the NCAA Tournament's Sweet 16. This unlikely achievement resulted in a head coaching opportunity at Notre Dame, where he had a very auspicious 20-year career before joining ESPN.

Historically, Fran Dunphy's career is very significant in terms of the Ivy League Golden Age narrative even though he didn't become the coach at Penn until 1989. No one else better represents the interconnection between Ivy League and Philadelphia Big 5 basketball. He played high school ball at Malvern Prep (Interacademic League) and college at La Salle (Big 5). Then he became a legendary coach at Penn (Ivy League) as well as Temple (Big 5). Consequently, he is the living embodiment of the rich tradition and heritage, which is Philadelphia basketball.

As discussed, the Big 5 itself is not a conference but rather an unofficial association of the five traditional

Philadelphia basketball powers: Penn, Villanova, Temple, La Salle, and St. Joseph's. It was begun in 1954 as both as showcase for Philadelphia's deep basketball talent pool, as well as a method of maintaining financial support for the Palestra's upkeep. In the post-war period, the Big 5 schools played all of their rivalry games at the Palestra, usually as doubleheaders. Since 1955, Penn has won 13 unofficial Big 5 titles, while hosting the city series at the Palestra during its most historic period (1954-1991). During the 1960s and '70s, Big 5 doubleheaders were televised on archaic UHF channels which required deft adjustments of the "rabbit ears" antenna. It was this period, the era of "Big 5 Fever"—which also paralleled the Golden Age of Ivy League basketball—that witnessed the most intense intra-city rivalries. It has often been said that anyone who does not appreciate the significance of winning the Big 5 title "is not from Philly"!

During the post-ESPN 1980s, television contracts began to heavily influence local Big 5 rivalries due to the need to appeal to national audiences. New conferences such as the Big East (Villanova) and the Atlantic 10 (Temple, La Salle, and St. Joseph's) were formed and the schools built new field houses in order to capture a larger share of the television revenue. Still, in 2013 the Big 5 tradition lives on and Penn, as a member of both the Ivy League and the Big 5, lies at its nexus. In addition, the Palestra as both "the cathedral of college basketball" and "the birthplace of Philadelphia's Big 5," holds a special place in basketball history.

As a player at La Salle, Dunphy was a member of the No. 2 ranked 1969 team which featured four NBA players: Larry Cannon, Ken Durrett, Bernie Williams, and Roland Taylor. This Tom Gola coached team also beat Penn that year in winning the Philadelphia Big 5 title. Twenty years later, Dunphy became the coach at Penn leading the team to two Top 25 national rankings between 1989 and 2006. He also compiled 310 wins at Penn, second in Ivy League history behind Princeton's Pete Carrill. In 2006, he became the coach at Temple, once again exhibiting the seamless symmetry between Ivy League and Big 5 basketball tradition.

Finally, the Philadelphian who is dean of all coaches (Big 5, Ivy League, NBA) is Dr. Jack Ramsay. Coach Ramsay, who holds a doctorate in education from the University of Pennsylvania, began his coaching career at his alma mater, St. Joseph's, in 1955. During his 12-year tenure he led the Hawks to five Big 5 crowns as well as 10 post-season NIT/NCAA appearances including the 1961 Final Four. He became a Hall of Fame coach after a long and illustrious NBA career, which includes his Portland Trailblazers winning the 1977 NBA Championship with center, Bill Walton. He also spent many years with ESPN as a commentator. At length, he was the pioneering career mentor that a cavalcade of Penn/Ivy coaches eventually followed to the NBA or ESPN including Jack McClosky, Digger Phelps, Dick Harter, Chuck Daly, and even van Breda Kolff himself. As with Fran Dunphy, Dr. Ramsay's career demonstrates the inextricable linkage between the Ivy League and the Big 5 schools with Penn at the center of this basketball solar system (see post-chapter table).

A more recent vintage of Philadelphia Big 5/Ivy League/NBA connections includes former mid-70s Penn All-Ivy Guard, Ed Stafanski, and St. Joseph's guard, Jim O'Brien. Stefanski was recently the general manager of the New Jersey Nets, while O'Brien was the coach of both the Boston Celtics and the Indiana Pacers.

Last but not least, another current ESPN analyst with a Philadelphia Big 5 background is Bill Raftery. Raftery was a star at La Salle in the early 1960s and was drafted by the New York Knicks. From the standpoint of sports media anthropology, the careers of Raftery, Digger Phelps, and Jack Ramsay are indicative of the historical influence that the "early Big 5/UHF rabbit ears" era broadcasts had on both the development of ESPN as well as basketball coverage generally as we know it today.

So with the foundational role of the University of Pennsylvania being deeply embedded within the context of American basketball history, where do Quaker teams rank among the Ivy Leagues all-time best? One methodology for rating the top teams across different time periods is a "body of work (BOW) analysis." This point ranking system is delineated as follows:

BOW Analysis		
Player Assessment Rating Points	**Peak Ranking Rating Points**	**NCAA Tournament Rating Points**
NBA All Star/ Champion Starter 5	Top 5 5	Final Four 5
NBA Significant Career 4	Top 10 4	Elite 8 4
NBA Roster Player 3	Top 15 3	Sweet 16/NIT Champ 3
NBA Draftee/ Ivy Player of the Year 2	Top 20 2	Round 2 2
All Ivy Consideration 1	Top 25 1	Ivy Champ 1

These criteria allow for the most comprehensive assessment of individual player talent as well as team accomplishment. The objective is to identify the best teams in Ivy League history in terms of individual player composition, the ability to compete on a national level (peak ranking) as well as in the NCAA Tournament. This methodology provides the capacity to separate the "Davids" from the "Goliaths" across the decades. Any team with a rating of 10 or more is a Goliath.

	Point Ranking Scale		
	Team	Rating Points	Key Players
#1	1971 Penn	23	Dave Wohl, Steve Bilsky, Jim Wolf, Corky Calhoun, Bobby Morse, Phil Hankinson
#2	1968 Princeton	20	Geoff Petrie, Joe Heiser, John Hummer, Chris Thomforde, John Haarlow
#3	1968 Columbia	19	Jim McMillian, Dave Newmark, Heyward Dotson, Roger Walaszak, George Starke
#4	1965 Princeton	19	Bill Bradley, Gary Walters, Ed Hummer, Robbie Brown, Bob Haarlow, Ken Rodenbach
#5	1979 Penn	19	Tony Price, Matt White, James Salters, Bobby Willis, Tim Smith
#6	1972 Penn	18	Phil Hankinson, C. Calhoun, B. Morse, Craig Littlepage, Al Cotler
#7	1967 Princeton	18	G. Walters, J. Heiser, J. Haarlow, C. Thomforde, E. Hummer
#8	1970 Penn	16	D. Wohl, S. Bilsky, J. Wolf, C. Calhoun, B. Morse

Point Ranking Scale			
	Team	Rating Points	Key Players
#9	1972 Princeton	16	Brian Taylor, Ted Manakas, Reggie Bird, Andy Rimol, Jim Sullivan, Bill Daake, Al Dufty, John Berger, Al Burton
#10	1975 Penn	15	Bob Bigelow, Ron Haigler, Ed Enoch, Ed Stefanski, John Engels
#11	1975 Princeton	15	Armond Hill, Tim van Blommesteyn, Mickey Steuerer, Peter Molloy, Barnes Hauptfuhrer, Brien O'Neil, IIan Ramati, Mark Hartley
#12	1973 Penn	14	P. Hankinson, B. Bigelow, R. Haigler, J. Engles
#13	1978 Penn	14	T. Price, M. White, J. Salters, B. Willis, Kevin McDonald
#14	1994 Penn	14	Matt Maloney, Jerome Allen, Ira Bowman
#15	1995 Penn	14	M. Maloney, J. Allen, I. Bowman
#16	1969 Princeton	14	G. Petrie, J. Hummer, C. Thomforde
#17	1969 Columbia	13	J. McMillian, H. Dotson, R. Walaszak, G. Starke
#18	1998 Princeton	12	Steve Goodrich, Mitch Henderson, Gabe Lewullis

Point Ranking Scale			
	Team	Rating Points	Key Players
#19	1976 Princeton	12	A. Hill, B. Hauptfuhrer, M. Steuerer, P. Molloy, Frank Sowinski
#20	2010 Cornell	12	Ryan Wittman, Jeff Foote, Louis Dale
#21	1970 Princeton	10	G. Petrie, J. Hummer, Bill Sickler, R. Bird
#22	2012 Harvard	Incomplete	Oliver McNally, Keith Wright, Kyle Casey, Brandyn Curry

Pre-Bradley Honorable Mention (Team and Key Players)	
1959 Dartmouth	Rudy LaRusso
1953 Penn	Ernie Beck
1951 Columbia	Jack Molinas
1946 Harvard	George Hauptfuhrer
1944 Dartmouth	Dick McGuire

Finally, Extending the BOW Analysis Methodology to determine the 20 best players in Ivy League history (including the pre-Bradley era), the results are as follows:

I. Ranking Criteria Ivy League	
All-American/Final Four/Top Round Draft	5
Ivy/Big 5 Player of the Year	3
All-Ivy Consideration	1

NBA Level	
Hall of Fame/Career 20 PPG or 10 RPG/Pioneer...	6
All-Star/Championship Team Starter	5
Rookie of the Year	4
Significant Career (5 years or more)	3
Roster Player	2
Draftee	1

II. Individual Player Rank (20 Best)			
	Player	**School**	**Points**
#1	Geoff Petrie	Princeton '70	30
#2	Bill Bradley	Princeton '65	26
#3	Rudy LaRusso	Dartmouth '59	25
#4	Dick McGuire*	Dartmouth '44	25
#5	Jim McMillian	Columbia '70	25
#6	Brian Taylor	Princeton '72	24
#7	John "Bud" Palmer	Princeton '45	15
#8	David "Corky" Calhoun	Penn '72	15
#9	John Hummer	Princeton '70	15
#10	Armond Hill	Princeton '76	15
#11	Dave Wohl	Penn '71	15
#12	Chris Dudley	Yale '87	14
#13	Tony Price	Penn '79	13

II. Individual Player Rank (20 Best)			
#14	Phil Hankinson	Penn '73	12
#15	Jeremy Lin	Harvard '10	12
#16	Ernie Beck	Penn '53	12
#17	Matt Maloney	Penn '95	11
#18	Steve Goodrich	Princeton '98	10
#19	Jerome Allen	Penn '95	10
#20	Ryan Wittman	Cornell '10	10

*   WWII Transfer to Final Four team

Honorable Mention: Ted Manakas, Princeton '73; Bob Bigelow, Penn '75; Dave Newmark, Columbia '68; Walter Palmer, Dartmouth '90; Ron Haigler, Penn '75; Pete Campbell, Princeton '62; Steve Bilsky, Penn '71; Gary Walters, Princeton '67; Hayward Dotson, Columbia '69; Perry Bromwell, Penn '87; Craig Robinson, Princeton '83; James Blackwell, Dartmouth '94; Ira Bowman, Penn '96; Joe Carrabino, Harvard '85; Chris Young*, Princeton '02; Zach Rosen, Penn '12; Keith Wright, Harvard '12; Ed Hummer, Princeton '67; Earl "Butch" Graves, Yale '84; Jeff Foote, Cornell '10; James Brown, Harvard '73; Floyd Lewis, Harvard '73; Saul Mariaschin, Harvard '47; Joe Heiser, Princeton '68; Chris Thomforde, Princeton '69.

*   Played Major League Baseball

Harvard's George Hauptfuhrer would have been included among the top 10, but for the fact that he chose to forgo an NBA career.

Ivy League		Nexus of Ivy League / Big 5 Basketball History		Big 5	
Princeton		**Penn**		**Villanova**	
NBA Players	10	NBA Players	12	NBA Players	39
Top 10	5	Top 10	5	Sweet 16	16
Top 25	8	Top 25	9	Elite 8	12
Sweet 16	3	Sweet 16	5	Final Four	5
Elite 8	2	Elite 8	3	National Champ	1
Final Four	1	Final Four	1	Big 5 Champ	25
Ivy Champ	26	Ivy Champ	25*		
		Big 5 Champ	13*	**Temple**	
Columbia				NBA Players	33
NBA Players	5			Sweet 16	7
Top 10	1			Elite 8	5
Top 25	3			Final Four	2
Ivy Champ	1			Big 5 Champ	20
Dartmouth				**St. Joseph's**	
NBA Players	6			NBA Players	17
Sweet 16	3			Sweet 16	7
Final Four	2			Elite 8	2
Ivy Champ	3			Final Four	1
				Big 5 Champ	19
Yale					
NBA Players	3	*Including Ties		**La Salle**	
Ivy Champ	3			NBA Players	22
				Sweet 16	2
Cornell				Elite 8	2
NBA Players	2			Final Four	2
Top 25	1			National Champ	1
Sweet 16	1			Big 5 Champ	9
Ivy Champ	4				
Brown					
NBA Players	2				
Ivy Champ	1				
Harvard					
NBA Players	4				
Top 25	1				
Ivy Champ	2				

Ivy League Coaches Timeline

I. PRINCETON

Butch van Breda Kolff (1962-1967)
- Record 103-31, Best Rank #3
- Los Angles Lakers Head Coach

Pete Carril (1967-1996)
- Record 514-261, Best Rank #8
- Basketball Hall of Fame, Springfield, Mass.
- Advisory Assistant to Sacramento Kings, Geoff Petrie

Bill Carmody (1996-2000)
- Record 92-25, Best Rank #8
- Head Coach, Northwestern University

II. PENN

Jack McClosky (1956-1966)
- Record 146-105, Best Rank: Ivy Champion
- Head Coach, Portland Trailblazers
- General Manager, Detroit Pistons (NBA Champion)

Dick Harter (1966-1971)
- Record 88-44, Best Rank # 3
- Head Coach, University of Oregon
- Assistant Coach, Detroit Pistons (NBA Champion)
- Head Coach, Charlotte Hornets

Digger Phelps (1967-1970)

- Assistant Coach (ESPN Analyst)
- Head Coach, Fordham University (Sweet 16)
- Head Coach, Notre Dame (Final Four)

Chuck Daly (1971-1977)

- Record 125-38, Best Rank #3
- Head Coach, Detroit Pistons, two time NBA Champion
- Head Coach, 1992 Olympic "Dream Team"
- Basketball Hall of Fame, Springfield, Mass.

Bob Weinhauer (1977-1982)

- Record 99-45, Best Rank #4 (Final Four)

Fran Dunphy (1989-2006)

- Record 310-163, Best Rank #11
- Head Coach, Temple University
- All-Inter-ac, Malvern Prep, 1966 (his transcendent accomplishment)

III. COLUMBIA

Jack Rohan (1962-1974/ 1991-1995)

- Record 198-247, Best Rank #6
- 1968 National Coach of the Year

IV. CORNELL

Steve Donohue (2000 -2010)

- Record 146-138, Best Rank #12
- Head Coach, Boston College

- Formerly Penn Assistant to Fran Dunphy
- 2010 National Coach of the Year

V. HARVARD

Tom Thibodeau (1985-1989)

- Assistant Coach
- Head Coach, Chicago Bulls (NBA Coach of the Year)

Tommy Amaker (2007-2012)

- Record 92-55, Best Rank #21
- Formerly Head Coach at Michigan and Seton Hall

VI. ST. JOSEPH'S (BIG 5)

Dr. Jack Ramsay (1955-1966)

- Basketball Hall of Fame, Springfield, Mass.
- Portland Trailblazers, 1977 NBA Champions
- ESPN analyst
- University of Pennsylvania, PhD

U.S. News and World Report 2012 University Rankings/Undergraduate I. Overall Rankings					
Ivies	Rank	Score	Highly Selective Non-Ivies with National Basketball Pedigree	Rank	Score
Harvard	1	100	Stanford	5	93
Princeton	1	100	Duke	10	92
Yale	3	98	Northwestern	12	90
Columbia	4	94	Vanderbilt	17	84
Penn	5	93	Notre Dame	19	83
Dartmouth	11	91	Georgetown	22	78
Brown	15	87	University of Virginia	25	76
Cornell	15	87	University of Michigan	28	75
			University of North Carolina	29	74
			Villanova*	1	NA

U.S. News and World Report 2012 University Rankings/Undergraduate II. Ivies (Ex Big 3) versus Top 5 Highly Selective					
Ivies / Ex Big 3	**Rank**	**Score**	**Top 5 Highly Selective**	**Rank**	**Score**
Columbia	4	94	Stanford	5	93
Penn	5	93	Duke	10	92
Dartmouth	11	91	Northwestern	12	90
Brown	15	87	Vanderbilt	17	84
Cornell	15	87	Notre Dame	19	83
Average	**10**	**90.4**	**Average**	**13.6**	**88.4**

*　　*Villanova is ranked #1 in the regional university category*

Basis for Comparison

1. <u>Skewed Results</u> - USNWR / Ex Big 3 is more representative...while Harvard, Princeton and Yale are <u>always</u> ranked #1, 2, 3; It is well understood that there is a "deck stacking effect" stemming from:

    A. <u>"The Dowager Countess / Rose Syndrome"</u> - In the PBS drama "Downton Abbey", the Dowager Countess (Maggie Smith) <u>always</u> won the Best Rose Contest <u>whether she deserved it or not</u>...because she was the Dowager Countess.

B. <u>Acceptance Ratio</u> - Is self-selecting and self-fulfilling, due to consistent desire of "high quality students" to attend one of the Big 3. If Prairie View A&M were ranked #1, its applications level would skyrocket...even if its high rank was not warranted by the quality of its educational offerings.

2. <u>"Much More Difficult to Get in than Stay in"</u> - Harvard, in particular, is known to have a less demanding undergraduate regimen.*

3. <u>"No Lock on Brains"</u> - Thousands of students who are selected by, or are qualified for, an Ivy university ultimately attend a highly selective non-Ivy university for a variety of reasons...and vice versa. For example, Chelsea Clinton was accepted at Princeton but, for her own personal reasons, chose to attend Stanford. Her decision provides <u>irrefutable empirical evidence</u> that the two schools are "at least equals". After all, Chelsea Clinton would never settle for second best!

Conclusion

There is no material difference between an Ivy university and a highly selective university with a basketball pedigree other than the level of academic brand equity and awareness. In financial accounting terms, this is known as goodwill. Therefore, the pool of NBA-caliber athletes with academic distinction (potential Bill Bradleys) should be pursued aggressively by Ivy admission committees. This will be discussed in greater detail in later chapters, but the bottom line is that a latter-day Geoff Petrie should be instructed in the advantages of playing basketball in the Ivy League. Despite the inability to award scholarships, Ivy "academic brand excellence" represents a unique and powerful recruiting tool for a select subset of top 100 basketball recruits, just as it did back in the Golden Age Era.

---

*　　In a new ranking system by <u>Alumni Factor</u> which focuses on student/ alumni assessments of undergraduate education quality, Harvard is ranked 37th...the Top 5 are Washington and Lee, Yale, Princeton, Rice and Holy Cross.

CHAPTER **5**

Geography Is Destiny? Northern Ivies versus Southern Ivies

> "If you want to know what Russia, China, or Iran will do next, don't read their newspapers or ask about what our spies have dug up—consult a map. Geography can reveal as much about a government's aims as its secret councils. More than ideology or domestic politics, what fundamentally defines a state is its place on the globe. Maps capture the key facts of history and culture."
>
> **– Robert Kaplan, STRATFOR,**
> **Defense Strategy Analyst**

Up to this point, the Golden Age of Ivy League basketball discussion has been a rather one-sided review of Penn and Princeton's basketball exploits with a dollop of Columbia's roundball bravado for good measure. An amateur cartographer might observe that all three of these Ivies lie south of Interstate Route 287 as it transverses Westchester County, New York. Running from the Tappan Zee Bridge, through White Plains and ending at the intersection of Interstate Route 95, just south of Greenwich, Connecticut; Route 287 represents a critical line of demarcation.

South of 287 lies "basketball country," a fertile ground rich in roundball talent, lore, and history. North of 287 lies "hockey country," a veritable frozen tundra in all things basketball. Stretching north toward Montreal and northeast toward Boston, hockey country is where the "Frozen Four," not the "Final Four," is decided. It is understandable then that Harvard, at the epicenter of hockey country, was also the locus of the greatest hockey movie ever made; the only romantic hockey movie ever produced. The movie, of course, is *Love Story*.

No greater distinction between Philadelphia's basketball culture and Boston's hockey culture can be drawn than that depicted by the movie's main character and hockey star, Oliver Barrett IV (Ryan O'Neal). As Oliver promenades across campus with his love interest, Jenny Cavilleri (Ali McGraw), his litany of impressive traits and accomplishments is laid bare to the movie audience: wealth, good looks, Harvard multi-generational legacy. However, all of these pale in comparison with his ultimate jock trump card. He informs Jenny that he is also, and most importantly, the star of Harvard's hockey team. In Boston, it gets no bigger than this.

For a moment, let's assume that we are the movie's director... yell "cut!"... and replay the scene. Then let's suppose that in the next take, after Ollie IV lists his impressive credentials, he finishes his soliloquy with the disclosure that he is the high scoring combo-guard on Harvard's basketball team rather than a hockey star. The effect on the movie audience would be stunned incredulity followed by laughter. Audience members would stare at each other quizzically while some might even begin to exit the theater. Thus is the distinction between ice hockey country (Harvard/Boston) and basketball country (Penn/Philadelphia).

I have a family member who had the (mis?)fortune to attend Harvard. Some years after graduation, she returned during February to attend a seminar with her husband. In looking for recreational activities to enliven their visit, they learned that Harvard's basketball team was hosting national power, Duke, that evening. Being good Philadelphia basketball fans, they were pleased to have the opportunity to see Duke play, but also resigned to the prospect that the game was probably sold out weeks in advance. After all, this was Duke and Lavietes Pavilion is rather small. Walking over to buy tickets, it was apparent that the parking lot was packed and thousands of fans were out to see an exciting sporting event. As they shuffled up to the ticket counter, they were shocked that there was no line and only a few hundred fans scattered about the gym. Then they heard a powerful crowd roar, not dissimilar to that heard when Tiger Woods sinks a 25 foot birdie putt on the final day of the Masters... Harvard's hockey team had just scored an inconsequential midseason goal against Rensselaer Polytechnic in the nearby rink, before a massive and rabid crowd.

Unfortunately, geography matters in Ivy League basketball history, but the recent years between 2007 and 2013 confirm that geography is not destiny. Harvard coach Tommy Amaker certainly agrees with this proposition. A former Big 10 and Big East coach at Michigan and Seton Hall, respectively, he had a strong belief in the basketball potential of a great Ivy League university, Oliver Barrett IV notwithstanding. Early on in Amaker's tenure, California recruit Oliver McNally joined fellow Californian and recent Knicks star, Jeremy Lin, to give Harvard respectability. Several years later, McNally teamed with Keith Wright and Kyle Casey among others to lead Harvard to its first outright Ivy League championship ever. It appears that many more may be in the offing if Amaker is given the opportunity to fully develop the program.

While being recruited, team captain McNally astutely observed that Harvard is the most famous school in the world and has had success in every field of endeavor that it has ever undertaken...except basketball?! Coach Amaker, himself a McDonald's All-American recruit at

Duke in the mid-80s, understands the potential for attracting high academic achieving, NBA-caliber recruits to Harvard—the same type of recuits that once proliferated in the Golden Age era. If Duke or Stanford can do it, why not Harvard? After all, Harvard has never been accused of considering itself inherently inferior to other institutions of higher learning, regardless of the task.

Prior to Harvard's 2012 title, Cornell, coached by Steve Donahue, executed a Pat Riley-esque 3-peat between 2008 and 2010. Donahue is another Philadelphia native who honed his skills as a longtime assistant to Fran Dunphy at Penn. Behind a nucleus of Ivy Player of the Year, Ryan Wittman, 7 foot center and future NBA player, Jeff Foote, and point guard Louis Dale, Cornell became the first Ivy League team in 30 years to reach the Sweet 16.

Ryan Wittman was the team's shooting star, both figuratively and literally. Pulling a name from the file of both legend and obscurity—a difficult trick—Wittman could be described as the "Rick Mount of Ivy League basketball." Mount, an Indiana schoolboy legend in the 1960s, was straight from central casting of the movie *Hoosiers*. Some in the state hyberbolically raved that he was the best "pure" shooter of all-time. At Purdue University, Mount did lead his team to the NCAA Finals in 1969 before losing to UCLA and Lew Alcindor. However, his overall game had certain limitations and he struggled at the NBA level. Still, "the man could shoot the basketball," as ESPN's Stephan A. Smith might say.

Likewise, Wittman is the fifth leading scorer in Ivy League history with 2,028 points. The son of Randy Wittman, University of Indiana star and later an NBA player and coach, his shooting skill and stalwart leadership were the driving force behind Cornell's consecutive championships between 2008 and 2010. Coach Donahue was awarded the Clair Bee Award as National Coach of the Year in 2010 and Wittman earned a BOW ranking among the Top 20 best basketball players in Ivy League history (that and $4 will get him an iced latte at Starbucks).

While recent "hockey country" success confirms that northern Ivies are not precluded from winning Ivy League basketball titles, the cultural hurdles still remain high. Unbeknownst to most basketball fans, a minor version of a "Linsanity" eruption occurred during April of 2012 in Madison Square Garden. However, this time it involved the New York Rangers rather than the Knicks. Twenty-one year old Chris Kreider, who one month earlier in March had been leading Boston College to the NCAA (Frozen Four) Hockey Championship, incredibly stepped into a New York Rangers uniform to score two game-winning goals during the Stanley Cup Playoffs.

Kreider has the usual hockey resume. Raised in Boxford, Massachusetts, he attended Masconomet Regional High School and prepped at Andover Academy prior to Boston College and the Rangers. As a child of "hockey country," he never had to wander far in order to maximize his potential. Kreider's path to success, while somewhat typical of the Boston area, would never happen in Philadelphia.

What happens to a great hockey player who is unlucky enough to grow up in Philadelphia is exemplified by the career experience of Ranger's Hall of Fame goalie, Mike Richter. Early on Richter went to Inter-ac prep school, Germantown Academy... a great place to play basketball, but hockey, not so much. Over time, it became apparent that in order to optimize his budding goal tending skills, it would be necessary to trek northward from basketball country into hockey country; and what better place to attend than Northwood School in Lake Placid, New York. Northwood is to hockey what Nick Bollettieri's Tennis Academy is to the professional ATP tour. Lake Placid is also the home of the Winter Olympic Training Complex, as well as hallowed ground of the U.S. Hockey Team's monumental upset of the Soviet Union in 1980. As Richter was passing around the Stanley Cup among his teammates after the Rangers' 1994 victory, he could rest assured that his boyhood sojourn, out of basketball country and up north to hockey country, was the best decision that he and his family ever made.

As the accompanying map (post-chapter) displays, basketball country extends southward from 287 to approximately the Washington D.C. beltway. Several miles south of 287 lies Mount Vernon, New York. Mount Vernon High School is the possessor of one of the nation's great basketball legacies. It has sent numerous players to the NBA including brother pairs Rodney and Scooter McCray, Gus and Ray Williams as well as former UConn star, Ben Gorden. Mount Vernon's Earl Tatum led Marquette to the 1977 NCAA Championship before joining the Los Angeles Lakers.

Traveling southward through the historical basketball hotbeds of New York City and New Jersey; then down the New Jersey Turnpike to Pennsylvania (Philadelphia and Environs) and through Delaware; one finally reaches Baltimore and D.C.

First, the state of Pennsylvania has had more Final Four participants (8) than any other state except Indiana (9). These include all of the Big 5 schools as well as Penn State, the University of Pittsburgh and Duquesne. In addition to being the home state of Wilt, van Breda Kolff, Pete Carril and Chuck Daly, it is also the location of a landmark representing a more contemporary basketball icon: the Kobe Steakhouse on City Line Avenue. Among Philadelphians, it has long been accepted wisdom that father, Joe Bryant (La Salle/76ers), named his son in honor of this fine epicurean temple. Again, as Stephen A. Smith might say, "The man loves his steaks!".

Next, Baltimore is the nation's lacrosse capital. It is

also the home of Dunbar High School, one of the nation's historic basketball programs. The 1982-1983 Dunbar Poets (namesake Edgar Allen Poe) are still considered by many to be the greatest team in high school basketball history. Their two year record was 59-0...only three games were even marginally competitive. The Poets were comprised of future NBA stars Reggie Williams (Clippers), Reggie Lewis (Celtics) David Wingate (76ers), and Tyrone "Muggsy" Bogues (Hornets). One of the grand and juicy ironies of basketball lore is that Muggsy Bogues was considered by his teammates, coaches, and college scouts to be by far the most dominant player on this great Dunbar team. However, unlike 7'1" Wilt Chamberlain at Overbrook High School or 7'2" Lew Alcindor at Power Memorial, Muggsy Bogues was only 5'3" tall.

Finally, one reaches the D.C. Beltway. "Inside the Beltway" is renowned for more than politics. Washington's Catholic League, personified by DeMatha, as well as city and suburban public schools, are the seedbed for many legendary players including Elgin Baylor, Dave Bing, Grant Hill, Kevin Durant and Harvard Coach, Tommy Amaker. In circuitous fashion, the source of "hockey country" renewal—Harvard Coach Amaker—has his roots in "basketball country"...as it should be.

The geographic significance of the hockey/basketball country dichotomy remains in place today and may be even stronger than ever. Patrician DeMatha and parvenu Oak Hill Academy are perennial stalwarts. New Jersey-based St. Anthony's and St. Benedict's are consistent powers. Of the Top 10 high school teams in the East ranked by *USA Today* in 2013, all are located south of Route 287.

An additional cultural and historical curiosity is the success of Ivy League universities in football, regardless of their geographic location. While Penn and Princeton have longstanding football traditions, Harvard, Yale, and Dartmouth are equal claimants to the fictional title of "Cradle of Football History in America."

Penn's Franklin Field was the first football stadium built in 1895. Harvard Stadium and the Yale Bowl followed in 1903 and 1914, respectively. Princeton played the first game versus Rutgers in 1869. Yale's Walter Camp was responsible for establishing the rules of modern American football. Harvard and Yale played the most famous game in Ivy League history in 1968. Down by three touchdowns in the second half, an undermanned Harvard team rallied back to score 16 points in the final two minutes to defeat No. 7 ranked Yale, 29-29. It was the only tie game in football history that actually resulted in a victory, as the accompanying newspaper headlines chronicled: "Harvard Wins 29-29!".

The Golden Age years of 1964 to 1979 were also glory years for Ivy League football. During this period, Yale—led by future Dallas Cowboy great, Calvin Hill, and Doonsberry legend, Brian Dowling—was a Top 10 ranked team. Cornell's Ed Marinaro was a close second in the 1971 Heisman Trophy voting. As consolation, he went on to star for the Minnesota Vikings and play in the Super Bowl before later becoming a TV star on the popular drama *Hill Street Blues*. Dartmouth, under the great Coach Bob Blackman, fielded a series of Top 25 ranked teams and won 12 Ivy League football titles between 1962 and 1982. The football training and discipline instilled in Dartmouth players Hank Paulson (U.S. Treasury Secretary) and Jeff Immelt (CEO of General Electric) certainly aided their later career development. Princeton stars during the Golden Age included Ivy League champion team standouts Cosmo Iacavazzi and Scott MacBean as well as New York Jets running back Hank Bjorkland.

Ivy universities are noted for their vast endowments. However, a lesser known micro-funding source is entitled the "endowed coaching position." In 2000, the aforementioned former Treasury Secretary and Goldman Sachs chairman, Hank Paulson, established the Robert L. Blackman endowed coaching position, honoring his former coach with a $2 million dollar gift. In a recent Wall Street Journal interview, Paulson was quoted as follows, "It was only when I look back after having spent time in the financial and business world that I realize how much I had learned...from him, in terms of life's lessons." Paulson was an offensive lineman at Dartmouth between 1965 and 1967.

As the following table delineates, Ivy League football success, unlike basketball and hockey, is not subject to geographical or cultural influences:

Ivy League Combined Championships* (Including Ties) I. Basketball Country Schools		
	Football	Basketball
Penn	16	25
Princeton	8	26
Columbia	1	2
TOTAL	**25**	**53**
Per School Average (excluding Columbia)	**12**	**25.5**

II. Hockey Country Schools		
	Football	**Basketball**
Harvard	13	2
Yale	15	4
Dartmouth	15	3
Cornell	3	4
Brown	4	1
TOTAL	**50**	**14**
Per School Average	**10**	**2.8**

*   **Through 2013**

Conclusion

The data clearly display that there is no significant geographical difference among Ivies in terms of football success; whereas, there is an overwhelming geographical difference in terms of basketball success.

A similar analysis could be undertaken regarding the hockey success of "basketball country" schools. Suffice it to say that this analysis would be rendered moot as Princeton is a perennial hockey afterthought, and Penn and Columbia don't even sponsor hockey teams.

So the question is, "has the Penn-Princeton basketball hegemony ended and been superseded by a 21st century league-wide basketball renaissance?". Cornell and Harvard have won five of the last six Ivy championships. In 2012, the Ivy League had two players in the NBA, Harvard's Jeremy Lin and Cornell's Jeff Foote. While the Zack Rosen-led Penn and Ian Hummer-led Princeton teams remain strong, recent indicators suggest that the future distribution of Ivy League basketball championships will begin to correlate with the past distribution of Ivy League football championships. Given the academic and institutional advantages of the New England Ivies, there is no reason that the basketball renaissance, which began in 2007 with the arrival of Coach Amaker, should not continue well into the future if, and it's a big if, Harvard as an institution stands behind the effort.

Penn and Princeton have distinct historical, cultural,

and geographical advantages when it comes to developing a nationally competitive basketball program. However, basketball is not football, and geography is not destiny. Two or three academically precocious ESPNU Top 100 recruits with NBA potential, but also long-term secular career vision (similar to Bill Bradley), are enough to achieve national recognition. While the likelihood of attracting academically qualified recruits at Bradley's basketball talent level (Top 10 nationally) is obviously remote, the likelihood of attracting 21st century, career focused recruits at the talent level of: Gary Walters, Chris Thomforde, Ted Manakas, Corky Calhoun, John Hummer, Jerome Allen, Ryan Wittman, or Zack Rosen (Top 100 nationally) is not. Such players are extant in the recruiting universe and should not be automatically conceded to Duke, North Carolina, et al. Former NBA player, Alvin Williams (Germantown Academy, Villanova, Raptors), is now an executive for player development with the Toronto Raptors. In a recent interview, he explained that it is only after a player signs his second NBA contract that the prospect of long-term financial security is even remotely realistic. Hence, the attraction of having an Ivy degree in one's back pocket.

In an age when post-graduate employment opportunities are rapidly diminishing, the Ivy League has too much to offer! The probability of a significant (greater than 5 year) NBA career is extremely low for most Top

100 ESPNU recruits. Multi-million dollar contracts are only available to those players who, after a several year competitive gauntlet, have established themselves as long-term NBA contributors... a very small coterie. Even future Geoff Petries and Brian Taylors understand that an Ivy degree is considerably more valuable than an Elite 8 appearance. If, due to injury or other circumstances, they are not able to attain a long-term NBA career, their Ivy degrees may provide opportunities in law, medicine, management, venture capital, or the media. Who knows? ... Under the right circumstances one might even land a Cabinet post as, say, Secretary of Education, like Harvard's Arne Duncan.

To close on a note of optimism, Harvard can succeed in basketball! Despite its geographic and academic disadvantages (too cerebral or too clever by half?), the university has the leadership in place necessary to enhance the basketball stature of the entire Ivy League. Specifically, Coach Amaker has been a McDonald's All-American and college player at Duke. He has coached in the Big 10 and Big East. He knows how to attract academically qualified, NBA-caliber recruits (and they are out there...witness Gerald Henderson, Wayne Ellington, Landry Fields, Jeremy Lin, Brook and Robin Lopez, Kyle Singler, Matt Carroll, and many others). After all, is Durham, North Carolina an inherently more attractive place to spend one's college years than Boston? I don't think so! The University of Virginia or Stanford can offer scholarships, but Harvard has a $30 billion endowment. Vanderbilt has an extensive alumni network. Harvard does not? Duke and North Carolina have elite basketball brands. Harvard trumps that with a unique brand of its own (and as a Princeton grad it pains me to say this)—the greatest academic institution in the world (its undergraduate school notwithstanding). World peace, manned space flight, nuclear fusion, and curing cancer are hard…basketball is not. Harvard, with unlimited human capital and financial resources, should be able to continue to compete at an elite (Top 25) level.

One final note of optimism. Boston is also the home of the greatest basketball franchise and symbol in history: the Boston Celtics. Since 1946 when Harvard's basketball fortunes began to languish, the Celtics have flourished…in Boston! Oliver McNally's sentiments are correct. If Harvard can be successful in everything else, it can also be successful in basketball. Here's hoping that coaches like Tommy Amaker, Jerome Allen, and Mitch Henderson can lead the Ivy League, if not back to the Golden Age, at least forward by expanding the scope of the basketball renaissance which began in 2007. With appropriate institutional support and inspiration from Jeremy Lin, this is a realistic possibility.

Post-script

The Northern/Southern, south of Route 287 jinx occurred again in 2013 as league leader, Harvard, ventured south to secure its second consecutive championship. Similar to an airplane entering the "Bermuda Triangle", Harvard lost on successive evenings to Princeton at Jadwin Gym and Penn at the Palestra. However, this time the basketball gods were smiling on Harvard. The following week, Princeton ventured north into Hockey Country and lost on successive evenings at Yale and Brown, giving the 2013 Ivy crown to Harvard.

Then, despite the earlier loss of its two best players, Kyle Casey and Brandyn Curry, this youthful Harvard team won its first round NCAA Tournament game versus nationally-ranked New Mexico, 68-62. Therefore, in the upcoming 2013-2014 season, Harvard could be ranked among the elite Top 25 once again, assuming that Casey and Curry rejoin the lineup of young, developing players. Finally, as a testament to "hockey country", Yale returned to the Frozen Four for the first time since 1952 and won the 2013 National Hockey Championship.

Basketball/Hockey Country

CHAPTER 6

The Arrival of the Black All-Americans

"Princeton in the nation's service"; the rise of John F. Kennedy's "Harvard whiz kids"—in 1965, the Ivy League celebrated leadership, not diversity. Ben Franklin (Penn), James Madison (Princeton), and Franklin D. Roosevelt (Harvard) were among the many Ivy stewards who guided our nation from its incipient colonial roots to its destination as the leading world power at the time of Bill Bradley's graduation. By opting to pursue a Rhodes Scholarship rather than enter the NBA immediately, Bradley was merely choosing to continue the longstanding tradition of leadership that Ivy institutions sought to imbue among their graduates. It is in this sense that the title of this chapter is "a red herring." It implies that black All-American recruits were absolutely critical to the rise of Ivy League basketball stature during the Golden Age (true)…but that would be missing a pivotal point which I will explain later.

There are many parallels and distinctions connecting

Princeton's Bill Bradley and Columbia's Jim McMillian. Obvious distinctions first: Bradley is white and McMillian is black; Bradley is from Crystal City, Missouri and McMillian is from Brooklyn, New York; Bradley is the product of an upper middle class upbringing while McMillian is from a family of lesser means. However, it is the parallels permeating the fabric of these two men that beget their commonality.

Bill Bradley was the first Top 10 national level basketball recruit to attend an Ivy League university. In fact Duke, not Princeton, was expected to be Bradley's first choice, but he decided that Princeton would provide a "superior platform" for the pursuit of his life goals which included a Rhodes Scholarship, politics and national leadership. This Princeton academic recruiting advantage, which existed in 1961, is even more evident today as virtually all of our nation's recent Presidents and Supreme Court Justice selections are Princeton, Harvard and Yale alums at the undergraduate or graduate level. For example, President Barack Obama and Governor Mitt Romney share three Harvard degrees between them. In addition, many of our national business leaders are Princeton and Dartmouth alums at the undergraduate level as well as Penn, Columbia and Harvard alums at the graduate level. Cornell and Brown graduates are also well represented in the categories of business and politics.

While Bill Bradley was the Ivy League's first Top 10,

NBA-caliber recruit, Jim McMillian was the first Top 10, NBA-caliber recruit who happened to be black. Here the distinctions end and the parallels, which revolve around leadership, begin. One of the key tenets of the Ivy League admission process is to seek out and identify those applicants possessing extraordinary leadership potential, both on the playing field and prospectively in life. Like Bradley, Jim McMillian was identified as such. In a societal context, it was apparent by 1966 that the nation's next generation of leaders would be multi-racial and it was the Ivy League's aspirational role to nurture as many future leaders as possible "regardless of race, color or creed." In 1966 Jim McMillian, Geoff Petrie and John Hummer (all future NBA 1st round draft selections) were admitted to their respective Ivy League schools on the basis of their academic and leadership potential. The fact that they were white/black or possessed NBA-caliber basketball talent, while not entirely incidental, was beside the point. All three young men had the foundational underpinnings necessary to be representative of the nation's next generation of leaders. As a suggestion to Coach Amaker and other current Ivy coaches regarding the admission process, one might ask if elite (ESPNU Top 100) basketball talent is considered to be a reason "to exclude" a young man from the admission pool in 2013. It should not be, and coaches should aggressively deploy the leadership examples from the Golden Age to drive home this point to their respective admission committees (see post-chapter: Ivy Pantheon of Leadership Beyond the Hardcourt).

Jim McMillian was not only the first black McDonald's level All-American to enroll at an Ivy League school, but he was arguably the best black player in Ivy League history (McMillian is #4 on the BOW rating scale and Brian Taylor is #5). Much as Bradley had done for Princeton, McMillian catapulted the Columbia program from obscurity to national prominence by his sophomore year (with the able assistance of teammates Dave Newmark, Hayward Dotson, Roger Walaszak and George Starke). Like Bradley, McMillian possessed a superlative all-around game. As previously discussed, he was an excellent scorer, defender and rebounder. He was an unselfish team player who could have easily padded his statistics to the possible detriment of his team. But similar to the great Bill Russell, he chose not to. In this sense he possessed sterling character traits applicable to both life and the hardcourt: he was a pioneer; he was a winner; and most of all, he was a leader.

It was not surprising then that, again like Bradley, championship success seemed to be hardwired in McMillian at both the NCAA and NBA level. At Columbia, he was the leader of a team that wrenched away the Ivy championship "strangle hold" maintained by the great Princeton teams of the 1960s. The 1968 titanic battles between Princeton (Petrie, Hummer, Heiser, Haarlow and Thomforde) and Columbia were epic. The 1968 national rankings (Columbia No. 6, Princeton No. 8) were indicative of the elite level of play by these two Ivy League goliaths. Geoff Petrie may have been the best player in Ivy League history (#1 BOW rating), but Jim McMillian was usually the winner of their key head-to-head matchups.

At the NBA level, both Bradley and McMillian were the third leading scorers on their respective championship teams. Bradley's Knicks won the 1970 and '73 NBA championships while McMillian's Lakers won the 1972 championship. Not only did the '72 Lakers win a record 33 games in a row, but the winning streak surreally began the day that McMillian replaced aging Hall of Famer, Elgin Baylor, in the starting lineup...yes, at one point, McMillian was an unthinkable 33-0 as an NBA starter! Such an accomplishment even makes Usain Bolts' metrics appear routine. Bradley played ten years of unselfish, team-oriented basketball averaging 12.4 ppg. McMillian played nine years of unselfish, team-oriented basketball averaging 13.8 ppg.

A demonstration of Bradley's self-effacing initiative was provided by his sojourn to Philadelphia's famed Charles Baker Summer League following his rookie season in 1968. As a small forward at Princeton, Bradley had developed into the seventh greatest player in college basketball history (ESPN Ranking). Yet, as a rookie with the Knicks, it became apparent that in the NBA, at 6' 5", he was an undersized and ineffective small forward. In an effort to retool his game and develop his skills as a two guard, Bradley spent his summer off-season enhancing his playmaking ability with the same rigor he had applied to his Rhodes Scholarship studies during the previous two years. His Baker League travails paid off handsomely and by 1970 he was the combo-guard complement to the Knicks' brilliant point guard, Walt Frazier...the rest is NBA history. The point is that a deified Rhodes Scholar was readily willing to address his deficiencies and work to improve his game to the benefit of his team, teammates and fans in New York City. A leader does not rest on his laurels. Rather, when a problem is identified, a leader endeavors to find a solution. An inch taller and 20 pounds heavier, McMillian had no problem making the transition to small forward in the NBA. However, throughout his career, like Bradley, he consistently adjusted his game for the betterment of the team and to the detriment of his individual statistics. Again, this is an inherent sign of maturity and leadership.

The Golden Age pursuit of scholar/athletes with leadership potential—who incidently happened to have NBA –caliber basketball skills—is directly applicable to the Ivy Leagues' mini-renaissance (2007-2013).Current basketball recruiting at its base-level is essentially identical to the Golden Age (i.e., if a Lew Alcindor or Anthony Davis is unsigned, try to sign him for goodness sake!) However, modern recruiting techniques are significantly more stratified, granular and computer-driven.

There are currently three subsets of elite recruits and, I would suggest, potentially a fourth. They could be characterized as follows:

1) <u>Top 10 National Recruits</u>—the "one and done, can't miss" NBA-caliber recruit personified over the decades by the likes of Oscar Robertson, Lew Alcindor, Bill Walton, Michael Jordan, Kobe Bryant and LeBron James. With the exception of Bill Bradley (and possibly Petrie and McMillian), these recruits have been historically out of reach for Ivy League schools primarily due to the fact that the prospect of deca-million dollar combined annual compensation is very high (0.9 probability, a Greg Oden injury not withstanding...1.0=100%). Even the possession of an Einstein-esque 170 IQ would not incline them toward Ivy enrollment. Besides, in 2013 it appears that nearly all one-and-done recruits have an exclusive arrangement to attend Kentucky (basketball power cum finishing school).

2) <u>McDonald's All-Amercians</u>—these include category 1 above , as well as approximately 15 other players (usually of high character and integrity due to the McDonald's screening process) just below the one-and-done category. Some examples of this type of

recruit over the years are Corky Calhoun, Brian Taylor, Kevin McHale, Danny Ainge, Christian Laettner, Grant Hill and J.J Reddick. Surprisingly, McDonald's All-Americans have only a 0.3 probability of achieving a significant NBA career (>5 years and signing a second multi-year contract). This is important because anything less than a significant NBA career does not provide for long-term financial security. Therefore, an Ivy degree would represent an attractive inducement for most academically qualified McDonald's All-Americans.

3) ESPNU Top 100-Rivals Top 150—these include categories 1 and 2 above as well as the next level (125) of recruits as identified by various screening services. Also known as the "best of the rest," these residual 125 have less than a 0.1 probability of achieving a significant NBA career. Therefore, virtually all of this category should be interested in the prospect of an Ivy degree, assuming they possess the requisite academic skills and leadership potential.

4) The Global Ivy 30—this category is a distillation of all of the above plus judicious scrutiny of the international player environment. Each year approximately 30 players could be culled from the top 150 as well as from international competition. The key benchmarks would be their academic/leadership credentials and basketball talent level. Of this recruiting subset of 30,

approximately 25 would fit into the ESPNU 100/0.1 probability of a significant NBA career category, while approximately 5 would fit into the McDonald's level/0.3 probability of a significant career category. Most of the Ivy 30 will also be courted by schools such as Stanford, Duke, North Carolina, Virginia, Vanderbilt, etc. Historical examples of such players have already been discussed but, to reiterate, they would include all of the Ivy players ranked in the BOW Top 20 in Chapter 4 as well as the Ivy players listed as honorable mention. In addition, numerous players who did not attend Ivy schools would also fit into the Ivy 30 category. A comprehensive, multi-decade examination of the rosters of the previously mentioned schools would unearth hundreds of possible names, but for simplicity's sake, let's take the following 12 players as Ivy 30 prototypes:

- Gerald Henderson (Duke)
- Wayne Ellington (North Carolina)
- Grant Hill (Duke and Ivy legacy..father Calvin, Yale '69)
- Christian Laettner (Duke)
- J.J. Reddick (Duke)
- Alvin Williams (Villanova)
- Brook Lopez (Stanford)
- Robin Lopez (Stanford)

- Adanol Foyle (Colgate)
- Shane Battier (Duke)
- Landry Fields (Stanford)
- Matt Carroll (Notre Dame)

For good measure, let's make this a baker's dozen by adding Mike Miller, the former McDonald's and University of Florida All-American who made 7 of 8 three point shots to lead the Miami Heat to victory in the final game of the 2012 NBA Championship (stand aside LeBron). Also, let's not forget Stanford's Jason Collins (and twin brother Jarron) who became the first major sports athlete to openly declare his gay sexual orientation.

All of the above are current or recent NBA players and all have had significant NBA careers. Twelve out of fifteen were McDonald's All-Americans, while the remaining three were ESPNU Top 100 recruits. The question is -- could these players be attracted by the prospect of enrollment at Ivy schools today? They certainly are reminiscent of the NBA-caliber recruits who played in the Ivy League back in the Golden Age.

I would put forth the proposition that not only could such players be readily persuaded to enroll at Ivy universities, but this prospect could actually be more attractive to them now than at any time in Ivy history. This includes the Golden Age during which an elite basketball brand and Bill Bradley-aura were enticing high school

All-Americans such as DeMatha/Harvard's James Brown. Here is why:

1) Potential Ivy League recruits (Ivy 30) are extremely intelligent and logical...endowed with the capacity for critical analysis. The simple construct of a tradeoff between the probability of a significant NBA career (in the range of 0.1 to 0.3 depending on the individual player and subject to the vagaries of injury and other misfortunes) versus the probability of attaining an Ivy degree (approximately 0.95) is logically biased toward the selection of an Ivy degree. This highly sophisticated analytical exercise is a descendant of the Ben Franklin (Penn) aphorism better known as "a bird in the hand is worth two in the bush."

2) Ivy 30 recruits are highly career focused; steeped in the knowledge that future global economic conditions are precarious; and well aware that the economic value of an Ivy degree is higher than at any time in history(and increasing geometrically similar to sports franchise ownership...think Columbia B.A. = Yankee's fractional-share ownership). In addition, the relative value of all other degrees in terms of demand in the marketplace is declining versus the Ivies. In bond market terms, one would say that the "spread is widening" between the Ivies and the rest. (Recent headline: "Ph.D. now comes with food stamps" is

indicative of the poor job market for even advanced degree holders).

3) The half-life of the value of an Ivy League degree is significantly longer than that of degrees from most other national universities. The logical "Spockian" conclusion is that unless a player is a Top 10, one-and-done prodigy, pursuing an Ivy education translates into much greater odds of career success than any alternative path. We are currently living in an era of diminished job prospects, coupled with a very low probability of an NBA career outcome. In fact, if logic is applied – in a true Dr. Spock manner—almost all ESPNU Top 100 recruits (with requisite academic and leadership credentials) should leap at the opportunity to play Ivy League basketball and receive an Ivy degree.

4) The considerable tradeoff between full scholarship schools and Ivy financial aid packages is an offsetting hurdle which counterbalances the aforementioned Spockian logic. However, Ivy schools possess endowments and financial resources on a colossal scale. Financial aid packages have been substantially enriched in recent years. A customized financial aid package combined with the ever increasing "relative value" of an Ivy degree returns the efficacy of both Spockian logic and probability analysis to the forefront of the school choice decision. In other words,

any potential Ivy 30 recruit adept at critical thinking would be foolish not to strongly consider an Ivy opportunity.

Digger Phelps, as Penn's recruiting contact with NBA-bound Corky Calhoun, recounted that in 1968 the primary attractions for Calhoun were: the prospect of receiving an Ivy degree demonstrating academic distinction; the prospect of combining basketball with Rhodes Scholarship potential, (Princeton's Bradley, Columbia's Hayward Dotson, and Penn's John Wideman were awarded Rhodes Scholarships during the 1960's); and the prospect of playing Ivy League basketball at the sport's mecca, the Palestra. All of these considerations still provide a powerful inducement in 2013. Therefore, the calculus of Phelps' recruiting brief to Calhoun is just as relevant today.

So what recruiting strategy might be successful in generating a higher Ivy 30 enrollment yield? The experience of the Golden Age could be instructive as follows:

1) Deploy the fabulous Ivy alumni networks to great advantage. By freshman year of high school, Ivy alums could be performing a national (and international) dragnet for the purpose of identifying 100 scholar/athletes possessing the potential combination of ESPNU 100 basketball talent, academic excellence

and leadership qualities.

2) Having made an early identification, follow this cohort closely over the ensuing years as the original pool of 100 is winnowed down to a residual group—the Ivy 30.

3) Having established early and continuous communication in a "Phelps/Calhoun manner," inject Spockian logic and probability analysis into the recruiting discussion as a constant, reinforcing tutorial. Remember, the Ivy 30 are highly sophisticated and academically precocious—fully capable of appreciating the Ben Franklin wisdom of "A bird in the hand."

4) Lead with your best punch! While the Ivy basketball brand may have been diminished over the years, the Ivy academic brand remains unchallenged. As Coach Bob Hurley earlier recounted, Duke and North Carolina have patrician brands; they are basketball royalty. In addition, primary competitors for Ivy 30 level recruits have their own distinct advantages. The schools that will provide the Ivies with the most rigorous competition are as follows:

- Duke
- Virginia
- North Carolina
- Notre Dame
- Stanford

- Michigan
- Vanderbilt
- Georgetown
- Northwestern
- Villanova

Also, the Patriot League universities (Lehigh, Lafayette, Bucknell, Colgate, et al) offer modest competition.

Except for the Patriot League, all of the above have superior athletic brands vis-à-vis the Ivy League. In addition, they have many first rate students who possess Ivy level qualifications. Still, I would submit that Ivy 30 recruits would be significantly influenced in their decision-making process by the "ultimate trump card," an Ivy League degree and all of the possibilities suggested therein.

5) Take advantage of the "Linsanity," mini-renaissance trend. During the Golden Age, it was accepted wisdom—as Harvard's James Brown believed—that playing in the Ivy League and attaining an NBA career were not mutually exclusive. Provide recruits with more recent empirical evidence (Lin, Foote, Allen, Dudley, Maloney and Penn No. 11, Cornell No. 12, Harvard No. 21) that supports the argument that playing in the Ivy League can not only lead to participation in a nationally significant, Top 25 program,

but also avail one to the possibility of a significant NBA career. However, if the significant NBA career does not "pan out," another attractive career path (law, business, politics, finance, media, etc.) will be waiting.

The optimal Ivy recruit will possess three key attributes:

- Academic excellence
- Leadership qualities
- NBA potential (as indicated by membership in the ESPNU 100 subset...the Ivy 30).

Why did Grant Hill attend Duke rather than his father's Yale? Why did Christian Laettner attend Duke and not Harvard? (Incidentally, Yale center Chris Dudley's NBA career was superior to that of Laettner who was not only ranked the 12th greatest college player by ESPN but was also a member of the 1992 Olympic "Dream Team.") Why did McDonald's All-American Adonal Foyle attend Colgate and not Duke or North Carolina? (The reason—a close mentoring relationship.) All of these decisions are deeply personal. However, I would submit that no one better understands the litany of key considerations than Harvard's Coach Amaker. As a McDonald's All-American himself, Coach Amaker's fundamental understanding of an Ivy 30 recruit's values and mindset, combined with Coach Digger Phelps' advocacy skills, could eventually increase Ivy 30 yield.

In order for Harvard to maintain a reasonably consistent Top 25 national ranking (at least four years out of ten), it would be necessary to attract one Ivy 30 recruit every two years—or five per decade—complemented by a talented and capable supporting cast. Such a recruiting task is pedestrian; hardly on the scale of building a football program capable of competing against Alabama, as Vanderbilt is attempting to do. With their innate advantages all Ivies, especially Harvard, are capable of –-in the sentiments of Oliver McNally—basketball success. As in the Golden Age, the objective of top-level Ivy League players is not merely to lay down the gauntlet of competition versus Kentucky, but rather to assume a leadership role in their post-basketball life. In return, Ivy basketball should provide its future leaders with the opportunity to play for a nationally-ranked program and maybe in the NBA as well.

At the outset of this chapter, I referred to the chapter title as a "red herring" in that it was not really a discussion about basketball at all, let alone black Ivy League basketball players. Rather, it was a chapter about leadership traits and attributes, whether black or white. Martin Luther King Jr.—who lived and died during the Golden Age—urged our society to "focus not on the color of a man's skin, but on the content of his character." Ivy admission departments should keep Dr. King's words in mind when assessing prospective student applications. Just because an applicant, black or white, happens to be an ESPNU 100 recruit with NBA potential does not mean that he should be relegated to the "wait list," or even worse, to four years at Duke, North Carolina or Stanford.

The life of Martin Luther King Jr. personifies the fact that—assuming requisite academic qualifications—character traits and leadership potential are the most important components of a prospective student's application. From that standpoint, future Bill Bradleys and Jim McMillians should be actively sought out and not precluded from the rigorous admissions process. Who knows, if they don't make it to the NBA, they may turn out to be mere Rhodes Scholars. Be they white Rhodes Scholars like Bradley, Rick Stengel (Princeton) and Glenn Fine (Harvard) or black Rhodes Scholars like Hayward Dotson (Columbia) and John Wideman (Penn), a strong leadership dynamic is evident throughout the Golden Age Pantheon of Ivy League basketball elites.

Finally, the significance of the chapter title, "The Arrival of the Black All-Americans," is not in reference to the superlative basketball skills they brought to their teams. Rather, it is to highlight—with MacArthur Genius Award recipient, John Wideman, and 33-0 NBA champion, Jim McMillian, at the vanguard—the leadership traits and attributes that these scholar/athletes displayed at their respective universities and beyond. They were All-Americans in basketball and All-Americans in life.

Ivy Pantheon of Leadership Beyond the Hardcourt*

- Jim McMillian, Columbia '70 – Business executive, apparel industry.
- Bill Bradley, Princeton '65 – Rhodes Scholar, Senator, Presidential candidate.
- Hayward Dotson, Columbia '69 – Rhodes Scholar, NYC politics, mediator.
- John Hummer, Princeton '70 – Stanford MBA and Hummer Winblad founder, venture capital.
- Brian Taylor,Princeton '73 –Executive, Inner City Development Foundation, Los Angeles.
- James Brown, Harvard '73 – CBS Sports host, NFL Today.
- Armond Hill, Princeton '76 – Head Coach Columbia, Asst. Coach Boston Celtics.
- Floyd Lewis, Harvard '73 – Attorney, Washington D.C.
- Arne Duncan, Harvard '88 – Cabinet Secretary, Dept. of Education.
- Craig Robinson, Princeton '83 – Head Coach, Oregon State, brother-in-law of President Obama.
- Steve Bilsky, Penn '71 – Penn Athletic Director.

- Gary Walters, Princeton '67 – Princeton Athletic Director.
- Ed Stefanski, Penn '76 – General Manager, New Jersey Nets.
- Geoff Petrie, Princeton '70 – Two-time NBA Executive of the Year, President, Sacramento Kings.
- Chris Dudley, Yale '87 – 2010 GOP gubernatorial nominee, State of Oregon.
- Rick Stengel, Princeton '77 – Rhodes Scholar, Time Magazine Executive Editor.
- Dave Wohl, Penn '71 – Head Coach, New Jersey Nets.
- .Corky Calhoun, Penn '72 – Petroleum executive, Exxon.
- Craig Littlepage, Penn '72 – University of Virginia Athletic Director.
- Al Burton, Princeton '74 – Attorney and Judge, Chicago.
- Andy Rimol, Princeton '74 – Financial executive, leasing industry.
- Jerome Allen, Penn '95 – Head Coach, Penn.
- Roger Gordon, Princeton '73 – Attorney and Judge, Philadelphia.
- Barnes Hauptfuhrer, Princeton '76 –Investment Banker, Private Equity Partner.
- John Wideman, Penn '63 – Rhodes Scholar,

MacArthur Genius Grant recipient, Brown University professor.

- Glenn Fine, Harvard '79 – Rhodes Scholar, Inspector General US Dept. of Justice.
- Jeremy Lin, Harvard 2010 – Leader of the "Linsanity" cult movement, Houston.
- John W. Rogers, Princeton '80 – Founder, Ariel Capital Management.
- John Thompson III, Princeton '88 – Head Coach, Georgetown University.
- Tony Price, Penn '79 - Executive, Wall Street/ Insurance Industry.
- George Starke, Columbia '70 - 14 year NFL career and anchor of the Redskins 1982 Super Bowl offensive line.
- John Berger, Princeton '74 - CEO, Reinsurance Industry.

* 19 of the above listed players were either drafted by or played in the NBA.

Barbarians at the Foul Line		
Harvard	**Basketball Counterparties**	**Kentucky**
World-class academic leader	**Brand**	College basketball royalty
Academic patrician	**Leadership stature**	Roundball goliath
Instill leadership attributes while competing at a Top 25 level	**Basketball mission**	Win the NCAA national championship at any cost
Rhodes Scholars...leaving for Oxford by June of senior year	**Resultant educational output/product**	One-and-doners... leaving for the NBA by April of freshman year
U.S. News and World Report academic rankings	**Key media metric**	*USA Today* Top 25 basketball rankings
International alumni association	**Key recruiting network**	AAU coaching sycophants
Ivy 30	**Key recruiting cohort**	Future NBA lottery draft selections
New York Times/Sports Illustrated	**Media press agent**	ESPN
Private equity, hedge fund managed endowments	**Financial resources**	ESPN T.V. contracts/Nike equipment/logo sales
Harvard, Princeton, Yale	**NCAA related "Big 3"**	ESPN, AAU, Nike

Barbarians at the Foul Line		
Harvard	**Basketball Counterparties**	**Kentucky**
Digger Phelps	**Chief spokesman**	Dick Vitale
Golden Age of Ivy League basketball (1964-1979)	**Bygone era**	Adolph Rupp/pre-Texas Western era (1946-1966)

Recruiting Quote of the Year: "Me being in the used car business, and I will let you know this, the basketball (recruiting) business is 25 times worse than the used car business...it's not even close." - Aaron Harrison Sr. Father of Top 10 ranked twins, Andrew and Aaron Jr., who will attend the University of Kentucky in 2013-2014.

CHAPTER 7

The Venues: Jadwin's "Shrine" versus the Palestra "Mecca"

Ode to Sport

To ask why we play, to ask why we watch, to ask why we cheer...is to ask why the snow falls or ask why the wind blows...it is in our nature.

As earlier stated, Dr. James Naismith invented basketball in 1891; but let's digress. Ball sports of all varieties are an innate part of the human condition and, anthropologically, an inherent component of human culture dating back to prehistory. Whether it be round rock throwing as a paleolithic era hunting strategy, animal hair constructed "hackey sack" balls preserved in the archeological digs of ancient Egypt, or rugby-style matches conducted in 4th century B.C. Greece; playing ball has been a crucial part of man's endeavors throughout the ages.

The Monks of the Middle Ages - who also preserved civilization via their Dark Age scrolls - established ball games on a more sophisticated level by developing the forerunner of tennis in French monasteries during the 12th century. Originally a relic of handball, as tennis evolved it went through various stages morphing from a form of squash to court tennis. Later, "the Sport of Kings" was popularized during the 1500s by French royalty and exported to England. Over the next 400 years tennis evolved further and eventually resulted in the famous 1981 "War of Decorum" - John McEnroe versus the Wimbledon tennis umpires. As far as I know there is no definitive empirical data confirming that the evolution of "ball sport sophistication" is correlated with the evolution of boorish behavior. However, I would recommend such a study as a future Princeton senior thesis topic.

The forerunner of basketball was developed by the Mayan Indians who discovered that the thick sap of the "castilla elastica" plant would stabilize and become moldable after being boiled with the juice of the local "ipoomoea alba" vine. The resultant "bounce" got the ball rolling so to speak, leading ultimately to Dr. Naismith's decision to shoot it through a hoop in 1891.

The fact that "ball playing" of various sorts dates back nearly 5,000 years, and ball games parallel the anthropological development of humankind, suggests that sport is more than just "fun and games". Rather than a mere frivolous diversion, sport is a deadly serious, hardwired aspect of man's sociological development to be treated with respect at all levels of society - including Ivy League universities. Calls to deemphasize sport should be viewed with a jaundiced-eye as they may be followed by calls to deemphasize sex and breathing, or 16 oz. sodas. In addition, for Ivy League universities, sport is a significant element of their ancient heritage, passed down directly from Oxford and Cambridge during the 19th century.

Sport, and ball sports specifically, are a global phenomenon - witness international fútbol (or soccer as it is known in the United States). Within the context of the current multilateral geopolitical framework, basketball has become the 2nd leading team sport primarily due to its popularization via the Olympic movement (FIBA) and more recently by the NBA. Any activity with such a global reach is exceedingly significant and, as earlier stated, Ivy institutions, particularly Harvard, should actively pursue leadership and seek to avoid irrelevance.

In order to play sports, a venue is necessary. The civilized sport of tennis was accommodated by French King Henry IV's majestic "court" built at Fontainebleau in 1600. Aristocratic competition occurred there until the French Revolution in 1789. The University of Pennsylvania's Franklin Field was built in 1895, actually preceding the reconstitution of the modern Olympiad in 1896. In fact, a case can be made that the establishment of the Penn Relays in 1894 led at least indirectly to the modern Olympic movement, which transcends sport and rises

to the level of global political and diplomatic reciproca-
tion. Again, this is important and just because the NCAA
has devolved into a greed-driven, superfluous governing
body does not mean that Ivy administrations should be
distracted by the NCAA's "trivial pursuits", and abdicate
their historic role of international sports leadership.

As an early example of Ivy League sports leadership,
the 2012 Olympics in London exist in large part due to
the organizational efforts of Princeton history professor
William Sloane in 1895. Professor Sloane encouraged
four Princeton track team members to make the Atlantic
crossing and participate in these novel Olympic games.
The rest of the 1896 U.S. Olympic team consisted of a
small group from Boston; meaning that our first Olympic
team was comprised of approximately 10 participants versus the 600 who participated in the 2012 London games.

Also in 1895, the construction of Franklin Field set
off a "venue race" of sorts with Ivy universities at the vanguard. Similar to later, more substantive races - the race
for the atomic bomb during World War II or the 1960s
Space Race - the sports venue race was marked by the
post-Franklin Field construction of Harvard Stadium
(1903), the Yale Bowl (1914), Princeton's Palmer Stadium
(1914) and finally, the Rose Bowl (1923) in Pasadena,
California which was modeled after the Yale Bowl.

"Stadia" design was developed in ancient Greece and
has evolved from rather basic structures to the more

sophisticated elliptical design of the Roman Coliseum. Highly complex modern day versions are exemplified by Dallas' Cowboys Stadium as well as the new Giants/Jets MetLife Stadium. These modern stadiums serve as monuments to the sociological significance of sport in the 21st century global culture, as well as sport as a driver of geopolitical influence. The effort and resources that China has put into its Olympic program demonstrate the power of sport as an international diplomatic symbol. In addition, the modern Olympic movement represents an Ivy-inspired ideal to resurrect the Arthurian "chivalric code of honor" among nations, and promote good will and fair play among the global participants.

As the name Palestra indicates, gymnasiums date back to ancient Greece but, of course, basketball courts would not become the centerpiece of the gymnasium until the 20th century. When the University of Pennsylvania built its Palestra in 1927, it was considered to be a fitting symbol for a university that had pioneered the sport of basketball 30 years earlier. As such it served, in diplomatic terms, as a communications tool and manifestation of basketball leadership. With a seating capacity of nearly 10,000, the Palestra was much larger than other gyms or field houses of the era. Therefore, it was also a communication symbol directed at Penn's Ivy competitors conveying that they were relatively insignificant "bit players" in this new sport of basketball.

Princeton was among these bit players when it constructed Dillon Gym in 1944. Little did the university realize that in less than 20 years Bill Bradley would transform this obscure, oversized high school gym into a household name among sports fans. By Bradley's senior year Dillon Gym would be nearly as famous as the Palestra or Madison Square Garden; all due to the *New York Times/Sports Illustrated* media-hype which promoted the development of the "Dollar Bill" mystique and nurtured the "Bradleymania" craze.

After Bradley graduated in 1965, the Princeton community - both "town and gown" - moved forward with a diplomatic broadside of its own. Just as the U.S. Navy might maneuver a nuclear air craft carrier closer to shore in order to send a message via"gunboat diplomacy"; a powerful van Breda Kolff/Bradley-led Princeton basketball program was about to send a message to both Penn and other national basketball competitors. The message was that Princeton had established itself as an incipient basketball dynasty (at least according to the staff writers at *Sports Illustrated*). The symbolic vessel of this diplomatic broadside was the construction of Jadwin Gym, a multi-purpose sports complex with a 21st century design aesthetic. Looking like a gargantuan Buckminster Fuller geodesic dome that had just landed from Mars, and with a seating capacity of nearly 7,000, Jadwin was a spectacular demonstration of architectural grandeur and institutional basketball authority. The communication conveyed to Princeton's basketball competitors was unmistakable...the Tigers are big-time!

Jadwin was built between 1965 and 1969. Its funding came from a grant by the family of Leander Stockwell Jadwin, Princeton '28. Mr. Jadwin had been the captain of the track team and died tragically in an automobile accident shortly after his graduation. In 1965, the same year as Bradley's graduation, his mother gave a generous gift of $27 million (more than $200 million in 2012 dollars) of which $6.5 million ($60 million in 2012 dollars) was applied to the construction of a new gymnasium project. With ample funding in hand, the opportunity was there to make a major basketball statement (lay down the gauntlet, if you will). In poker terms, Princeton "called" Penn's Palestra Mecca and "raised" it one Shrine to the memory of Bill Bradley via the beneficence of Leander Jadwin and family.

By Bill Bradley's junior year, Dillon Gym had become besieged with overflow crowds of fans and press. With barely the seating capacity of a well-endowed prep school, remote closed-circuit television facilities had to be set up elsewhere on the Princeton campus in order to accommodate fan interest during the Bradleymania craze of 1964-1965...think Beatlemania without musical instruments. It appeared obvious in 1965 that, as a burgeoning, nationally significant basketball program, a new and expanded athletic facility would be necessary. With funding in place and alumni support solidified , construction on Jadwin began. By 1967 Princeton was still ranked No. 3 after defeating North Carolina. Then the key Golden Age catalyst (Bradley was the fuel and VBK was the match), Butch van Breda Kolff, departed for the Los Angeles Lakers and he was succeeded by Coach Pete Carril.

One of the leaders of the Princeton "town and gown" community at the time was highly regarded lawyer, Jack McCarthy, Princeton '43. One of Princeton's leading citizens (town) as well as an esteemed graduate of the university (gown), Mr. McCarthy was honored with the following effusive praise from former New Jersey Governor, Brendon Byrne: "Princeton is known as the home of three very famous people - Albert Einstein, Woodrow Wilson, and Jack McCarthy." In addition, as captain of Princeton's 1942 baseball team, McCarthy was an important supporter of Princeton's athletic program.

Coach Carril recently recounted that when he first nervously addressed influential Princeton alumni and dignitaries upon accepting this high visibility coaching position, it was Jack McCarthy who came forward to reassure him that success was in the offing. Thirty years and 521 wins later, McCarthy's reassurance to Carril was proven to be justified.

More than 40 years on, Jadwin Gym remains a

spectacular architectural structure. At first glance it appears to have been built within the past five years, mimicking other mega-venues such as the new Brooklyn Nets' Barclays Center. As Penn's Digger Phelps learned when recruiting Corky Calhoun in 1968, the opportunity to play at a perceived "exceptional venue" like the Palestra or Jadwin is an important consideration for a well-regarded young athlete. From that standpoint, a strong case can be made that Jadwin has helped to maintain the Golden Age/Bradley momentum (the house that Bradley and VBK built) and support Princeton basketball tradition and accomplishment down through the subsequent decades; just as the Palestra has done for the University of Pennsylvania.

In 2009, Coach Pete Carril was honored in a ceremony which designated the basketball facility at Jadwin as the new "Carril Court at Jadwin Gym" . Given his decades of service to Princeton basketball, the recognition is well deserved. Yet it is a sad state of affairs that the maestro of Princeton's symphonic march to dynastic acclaim and Goliath status, Butch van Breda Kolff, remains an underappreciated bygone figure in 2013. After all, even today the most prominent banners hanging over Carril Court at Jadwin are those representing the VBK dynasty years - Bill Bradley's 1965, No. 3 ranked Final Four team and the Gary Walters/Chris Thomforde 1967, No. 3 ranked Sweet 16 team...who knew?

In terms of the development of its basketball program, Harvard is approximately where Princeton was circa 1965 when Jadwin's construction began. In 2012 its team was a heralded Ivy champion with Golden Age-type, NBA-caliber players. Under Coach Amaker's leadership, Harvard is attracting top recruits with Corky Calhoun potential.

Anyone who respects the accomplishments of the "Golden Age Pantheon of Leadership" (Five Rhodes Scholars, a presidential candidate, a gubernatorial candidate, several cabinet members and numerous executives at the highest level of management) can only hope that Harvard President Drew Faust and Harvard's institutional leaders continue their support of Coach Amaker and his successful effort. At this point in Harvard's basketball evolution, a Jadwin-style monument might not necessarily be appropriate. However, the administration's continuing support of a job well done, and a noble mission worth pursuing, is definitely in order.

Footnote—Robert Goheen was the 16th president of Princeton University (1957-1972). He presided over the admittance of Bill Bradley and the construction of Jadwin Gym. When he retired in 1972, the Golden Age demise began...coincidence or causal?

Jadwin Gym
George W. Ford

CHAPTER 8

Dynamic Determinism: the Metamorphosis from Goliath to David

<u>Dynamic Determinism:</u> di-ʻnam-ik di-ʻter-men-iz-em:
1. **The process by which a confluence or prepon-derance of factors sets off a dynamic reaction which is determinative of future events and from which there is no recovery, 2. Point of no return, 3. Tipping point, 4. Crossing the Rubicon, 5. Up the creek without a paddle.**

Between 1968 and 1996 a "tipping point" was reached in the devolution from Ivy League basketball Goliath to David. This transformation involved a physical and psychological process. The metamorphosis required both the diminishment of physical capacity as well as a lowering of rational expectations. Before identifying the precise date of the transformation from Goliath to David, it would be useful to examine a pertinent timeline of Ivy

League basketball history. In this regard, the post-chapter charts delineate the key events in Ivy history from the first Penn-Yale game in 1897 to Harvard's first championship in 2012. However, in order to hone in on the specific date of "Goliath-to-David" transformation, I will divide the events along this historical timeline into five distinct parts:

I. **The Cappy Cappon Era (1938-1961)** - The origin of the label "Ivy League" is unknown and subject to numerous hypotheses. What is known is that the derivation of the name stems from sports and sporting activity; not the academic excellence, social pedigree or exclusiveness that is associated with the term today. There would be no such thing as modern-day "academic elites" were it not for the erstwhile sports gladiators, who adopted chivalry-related "old school" values and methods from Oxford and Cambridge back in the post-Civil War 1870's. The development of American football by the Big 3 (Princeton, Harvard and Yale) in the years between 1875 and 1900 followed by sports initiatives in track and field (Penn Relays and the Olympics in 1896) and basketball (Penn versus Yale in 1897), planted the seeds for the establishment of the Ivy League 60 years later. It is always useful to remind tenured professors, many of whom loathe Ivy sports tradition, that these traditions are the foundation of their very existence, as well as the prestige that has accrued to their respective universities. Without sports and the values that have been imparted over the past two centuries, there would be no such thing as an Ivy League and all of the supercilious "academic bragging rights" associated with it.

When it comes to Ivy League old school values, Coach Franklin C. (Cappy) Cappon espoused "old school values of the oldest sort". Coach Cappon was raised in a well-to-do Midwestern family, and was a spirited and successful college athlete at the University of Michigan. He later coached at Michigan before arriving at Princeton in 1938 to become its basketball coach. Some of Cappon's bedrock principles in terms of coaching strategies included:

- **The Iron Five** - Playing your 5 best players <u>without substitutes</u>...if your sixth man is not as good as your fifth, why play him?
- **The Five Man Weave** - Some might claim that Coach Cappon's "Famous Five Man Weave" eventually morphed into Coach Carril's "Famed Princeton Offense", but this is not necessarily so.
- **No Fast Breaks** - Coach Cappon believed that this "Helter Skelter, Bull-in-a-China-shop" activity <u>conveyed a lack of discipline</u>.

- **<u>No Uniform Changes</u>** - Princeton players wore the same-style basketball uniforms from Cappon's arrival in 1938 to Bill Bradley's arrival in 1961. Can one imagine the distress level of Nike marketing executives if Cappon's sartorial mindset were prevalent today in 2013? Better yet, can one imagine Coach Cappon having a discussion with the rapper, Jay-Z, about his incorporation of gang colors into the new Brooklyn Nets uniforms and logo schematic?

All told, as Princeton chronicler Seldon Edwards once wrote, Cappon's coaching style translated into "short white man's basketball at its best".

Another of Coach Cappon's bedrock principles was that <u>Princeton did not recruit</u>. Yet the ironic, serendipitous decision leading to the dawn of the Golden Age era was that Bill Bradley, despite dozens of scholarships from national powers such as Duke, sought out admission to Princeton for academic reasons. By selecting to attend Princeton without a scholarship, Bradley was also committing himself to play a brand of "Cappy Cappon" basketball that would have been unlikely to lead to a Final Four appearance and 30 PPG average during his senior year (so much for the "Dollar Bill" legend). It was only after the arrival of Coach Butch van Breda Kolff, with his fast-paced-NBA-style offense and effective recruiting, that Bradley's splendid accomplishments were made possible.

The seminal moment of the Golden Age of Ivy League basketball occurred during Bradley's freshman year when Coach Cappon died of a massive heart attack in the Dillon Gym showers. Subsequent to his death, Bradley was rudderless and Princeton basketball was without leadership and direction. At that point, part two of the Golden Age catalytic process occurred when Butch van Breda Kolff arrived to take the coaching reins. VBK had been a player at Princeton during the mid- 1940's. He then played for the New York Knickerbockers before becoming a successful head coach at Lafayette College, where he also coached Pete Carril.

II. **The Golden Age Goliath (1962-1975)** - The happenstance of Bradley's academically-based selection of Princeton, coupled with Coach Cappon's tragic and untimely death, resulted in the unanticipated pairing of Bradley and VBK. Neither man had ever expected this pairing and in most respects it was unsuited in terms of priorities and temperament. Yet, without each other's complimentary skills and talent, neither one would have achieved the legendary status that was their fate. VBK, as a former NBA player, unleashed Bradley from the shackles of the Cappon "five man weave" and introduced a full court, fast-breaking-style of play that was conducive to 30 PPG scoring.

VBK complained that Bradley lacked the intensity and "killer instinct" necessary to press the advantage. Still, with the full complicity of the New York sports media-complex, "Bradleymania" flourished, Princeton became an incipient dynasty and VBK became the head coach of a storied Los Angeles Lakers franchise, all within the space of five years. Ironically, two men whose paths were never meant to cross, became one of the most historic tandems in history. Along with Ruth and Gehrig, Rogers and Astaire, Magic and Bird; Bradley and VBK share a place in the Pantheon of Duet Legends.

By 1965, the legendary pairing of Bradley and VBK had resulted in the elite NBA-caliber basketball brand that would attract academically precocious high school All-Americans to the Ivy League over the next decade. Between Princeton's Final Four appearance in 1965 and Princeton's NIT victory in 1975, a parade of future NBA players and draftees would raise the national profile of Ivy League basketball to the highest level. However, by 1975 Armond Hill would be the last of the great Golden Age players still roaming the hardwood.

When Coach Pete Carril replaced VBK in 1967, the No. 3 ranked Tigers were stocked with NBA-caliber players and endowed with "elite brand equity", similar to Duke or North Carolina. However, as earlier discussed, the "spontaneous combustion" triggered by the unanticipated combination of Bradley and VBK was slowly beginning to dissipate. One by one, such "Magnificent Eleven" notables as Bradley, McMillian, Petrie, Hummer, Wohl, Calhoun and Taylor would graduate and by 1975 Armond Hill was the last "McDonald's level All-American" standing.

After a halting start to the 1974-75 campaign, Princeton, led by Hill, closed its season in strong fashion reaching a peak ranking of No. 8. However, its slow and inconsistent start resulted in yet another Penn Ivy League title and No. 7 peak ranking for the Quakers. Once again, Princeton would be forced to play "best man" to Penn's "bridegroom" and accept an NIT bid in lieu of an NCAA appearance.

Since his arrival as head coach, Pete Carril had struggled to sustain the VBK/Bradley legacy. He battled against extremely intense competition, first from Columbia in the late 1960s and later from Penn in the 1970s. In the eight year stretch from 1967-1975, Columbia and/or Penn were ranked in the Top 10 four times and in the Top 20 seven times. During this period Princeton had been able to recruit future NBA stars Hill and Brian Taylor, NBA roster player Ted Manakas as well as numerous future NBA draftees. Nevertheless, the afterglow of the post-Bradley era's prestige and media-hype had subsided to the point that the Ivy's Goliath, power conference image was increasingly on the wane.

As the 1975 NIT unfolded, Princeton would be facing very formidable competition from a series of nationally-ranked teams. The Tigers lineup of Hill, Barnes Hauptfuhrer, Tim van Blommesteyn, Mickey Steuerer and Peter Molloy would enter the field as underdogs to the likes of South Carolina, Oregon and Providence. In order to win the tournament, Princeton would have to defeat these ranked opponents in sequence. This was not a gauntlet to be run by the faint of heart.

Between 1968, when the Tigers were led by Geoff Petrie and John Hummer, and 1975 Princeton's physical capacity to match up against Top 10 competition had diminished. In order to defeat several ranked teams in succession, a cerebral/psychological component would have to be added to the Princeton strategic arsenal. This mental component coupled with the highly-disciplined Princeton offense - and hard-nosed defense - would all be necessary if the Tigers were to have any chance of winning the NIT. In addition, Princeton would have to assume the guise of "David" in order to summon the wiles and guile that would enable it to defeat a series of nationally-ranked teams and win the tournament.

III. **The Onset of David (1975)** - The NIT (National Invitation Tournament) was a much more significant event in 1975. The NCAA field consisted of only 32 teams, primarily conference champions. This resulted in many Top 20 ranked teams pursuing an alternative post-season venue, and that venue was the NIT at New York's Madison Square Garden.

Princeton had finished the regular season on a 9 game winning streak and arrived at the Garden with considerable momentum. A quality Holy Cross team coached by former Dartmouth mentor, George Blaney, was the Tigers' first opponent. Princeton won 84-63, but now had to face a powerful South Carolina team that featured future Denver Nugget Hall of Famer, Alex English, who scored 25,613 (21.5 PPG) points during his NBA career, the 13th highest in NBA history. At this point the Tigers tournament was expected to end, but an intense defense coupled with heady mistake-free play resulted in an 86-67 Princeton rout.

Next, an Ivy grudge match would unfold as Coach Carril and the Tigers would man-up to challenge the University of Oregon, directed by former Penn coach, Dick Harter. This Oregon team featured two future NBA stars, Ron Lee and Greg Ballard. The Ducks would be Princeton's highest hurdle of the tournament. If the Tigers could defeat Oregon, they could win it all. Unlike the two previous games, Princeton was never able to establish a lead. Oregon's defensive intensity matched theirs and the physical superiority of Lee and Ballard was difficult to overcome. Still, intelligent play, deft coaching and a peerless Armond Hill enabled Princeton to eke out a 58-57 victory. As a result, this game at Madison Square Garden <u>would signify a watershed moment in the history of Ivy League basketball</u>.

Princeton went on to defeat Providence, 85-69, to win the tournament. However, it was in the post-tournament celebration that one discovered the indications that a "Goliath to David" tipping point had been reached. First, the *New York Times* editorialized that Princeton's cerebral style of play - offensively and defensively - was to be admired for both its results as well as "the character that it demonstrated" (since when did the *NY Times* editorial page do sports reporting?). Next, an organic buzz effervesced throughout the campus suggesting that a more intelligent Princeton team had overcome more physically gifted opponents. This self-congratulatory "groupthink" observation was summarized in a "Princeton Alumni Weekly" article by Dan White, Princeton '65, on April 15, 1975.

In an extended tribute to Coach Carril and his NIT champions, White contended that "the rule of modern basketball is that a team must have giants to win...man for man the Princeton squad averaged 23 pounds less than Oregon, one of the most physical teams in the country, but Carril prevailed by stressing smart defense, patience, discipline and character". White further pointed out that, among basketball cognoscenti, it was self-evident that Coach

Carril had instilled in his team a level of intelligence and, therefore, provided the Tigers with a unique advantage. Throughout the Princeton campus a sentiment emerged that the Tigers had just dispatched four brutish teams consisting of Nike-clad neanderthals possessing low basketball IQs (or low IQs in general for that matter).

In a display of uncanny hubris, it wasn't enough for the Princeton community to attribute this stunning victory to: the burgeoning confidence of its excellent players, the powerful forces of momentum, and effective coaching. To the contrary, it appeared that the "academic ivory tower constituency" (certain professors, administrators and students...most of whom were not basketball fans to begin with) insisted on taking credit for this triumph by virtue of the fact that a small portion of their "keen intellect" had rubbed off on the Princeton players, pushing them over the line to victory. The irony of ironies was that the so-called "academic elite", who routinely denigrated Princeton athletics, were attempting to co-opt this NIT victory for their own purposes...who'da thunk it?

It was on this date then in Ivy League basketball history - the publication date of April 15, 1975 - that the Tigers became more admired for their intelligent, self-effacing, disciplined style of play than for the All-Americans who had comprised their teams (Bradley, Petrie, Hummer, Taylor, Manakas and Armond Hill). Yet, in this "David roll-out moment" it is convenient to forget that the

Princeton NIT champions were led by Hill, a quality NBA player during his eight year career. In this regard, the truer lesson might be that it is better to play smart, intelligent basketball with NBA-caliber players, than without.

Although the Penn program would hold out for another five years, the power conference trend line had definitely been altered. Just as the rest of the Ivy League had mimicked VBK and Bradley post-1965 by pursuing NBA-caliber recruits; now post-1975, the Ivies would eventually follow a more tactical and cerebral path...the Princeton model. David had been conceived and ESPN's Dick Vitale would be fulfilled 14 years hence.

IV. **The Last Stand of Penn's Goliath (1976-1982)** - A tipping point had been reached; Goliath was on the wane; the David seed had begun to germinate; still, it was early days and Penn Coach Chuck Daly apparently did not subscribe to the "Princeton Alumni Weekly". For the next several years Penn would continue its attempts to compete at the highest level, fielding NBA-caliber players. The result was that by 1979, even after Daly had departed to the NBA, Penn would eventually achieve its Final Four objective under Coach Bob Weinhauer.

1976 was the senior year for Princeton's Armond Hill, Barnes Hauptfuhrer and Mickey Steuerer. They were joined by future NBA draftee, Frank Sowinski, to form what would be the Tigers' final Goliath level team until 1998, when the No. 8 ranked Tigers would be led by Steve Goodrich, Mitch Henderson and Gabe Lewullis. Both the 1976 and 1977 Princeton teams defeated Penn to win the Ivy League championship. Subsequently, Penn would again win the next five championships between 1978 and 1983.

Penn's 1978 team displayed a combination of NBA talent and "deep depth". Team leader Tony Price was to become the last Golden Age player to make an NBA roster. In addition, James Salters, Matt White, Bobby Willis and Kevin McDonald were all NBA draftees. The teamwork and experience gained in 1978 would lay the foundation for Penn's 1979 Final Four run. With four returning starters from a No. 16 ranked team - McDonald had graduated - the 1979 Quakers breezed to another Ivy title.

Reaching the Final Four in any given year is exceedingly difficult and 1979 would prove to be no exception. Despite its hardened experience, Penn was seeded 9th out of 10 teams in the Eastern Regionals. Its first challenge would be Jim Valvano's Iona Gaels led by future NBA star Jeff Ruland. The Quakers prevailed 73-69 as the 6'7" Price scored 27 points and pulled down 12 rebounds. At this point Penn's tournament was expected to end as they faced No. 1 seed North Carolina, led by

Mike O'Koren and Al Wood. The game was played in Raleigh, North Carolina and Penn was considered to be a long shot at best. Yet, the Quakers survived 72-71, behind Tony Price's 25 points and 9 rebounds. Next up was Syracuse. After an 84-76 Penn victory Syracuse coach, Jim Boeheim, called Tony Price "the best forward we've seen all year"! Finally, in the Elite 8 Penn defeated St. John's as James Salters made a pair of free throws with 23 seconds left. The Final Four had been achieved and Michigan State with Magic Johnson awaited. Penn's good fortune would end...so would the Golden Age of Ivy League basketball.

The Wilderness Years (1980-2010) were to follow as the post-Bradley Ivy brand, and its accompaniment of NBA-caliber players, would fade to black. ESPN was in the process of re-packaging college basketball for the sports consumer and the Ivies were to play a new role in their theatrical cable TV narrative. The Ivy League's new role would definitely not be that of a Goliath-laden "power conference" on par with the ACC, as had been the case between 1965 and 1972. Apparently, even if Penn's Chuck Daly had not read Dan White's article in the "Princeton Alumni Weekly", ESPN and Dick Vitale seemingly had. Moreover, even as ESPN was hard at work transforming the Ivy brand from "Goliath to David," Ivy coaches were dealing with other issues.

Craig Littlepage, Penn's coach in the early 1980s, lamented that spiraling tuition costs (Penn went from $5,000 in 1972 to $60,000 in 2012) coupled with a lack of scholarships provided Duke and Stanford with an escalating recruiting advantage; especially as the post-Bradley brand was becoming a distant memory for players coming of age in the 1980s. Furthermore, the Digger Phelps/ Corky Calhoun "Rhodes Scholarship template" had lost recruiting currency as the AAU/Nike duo began to assume year-round, 24/7 control over promising young (and easily influenced) basketball players. As the 1980s were ending, the Ivy tradition remained but the talent level was no longer nationally competitive.

V. **Princeton Versus Georgetown and UCLA (1989-1996)** - Most basketball fans reading this book will be familiar with the outcome of the ultimate David versus Goliath matchup...Princeton versus No. 1 ranked Georgetown in 1989. Similar to the 1968 Harvard 29-29 football victory over Yale, on this March evening Princeton defeated Georgetown 49-50 in the first round of the NCAA Tournament. Unfortunately, since Georgetown lost on every level except the final score, Princeton was unable to continue on to the second round. Still for ESPN and the national sports media-complex, Princeton's "moral victory" could not have been more resounding.

In the three years prior to 1989, the Ivy League's NCAA representative had lost its first round pairing by a combined 120 points. This statistic is all the more shocking in that only 10 years earlier Penn had been in the Final Four. By the late 1980s there was even some discussion that the Ivy League did not merit an automatic invitation to the NCAA Tournament. With this in mind, let's follow the Goliath-to-David developmental sequence - from power conference to potential non-qualifier - between 1969 and 1989.

In the years circa 1970 (1968-1972) the Ivy League was a power conference comprised of nationally-ranked teams and marinated with first round NBA Draft choices. Penn's competition consisted of Princeton, Columbia, Harvard and Dartmouth...with even Yale and Brown providing some difficult moments. By 1975, Penn's only competition was Princeton.

By 1980, Penn had no significant intra-league competition. In fact, the demise of Penn's basketball program - in addition to the factors previously outlined by Craig Littlepage - was primarily precipitated by internal institutional paranoia. As of 1983, Penn had won 11 of the previous 13 Ivy League championships. It had been to several Sweet 16s and Elite 8s, as well as the Final Four. Its degree of Ivy dominance had become so uncomfortable for the University of Pennsylvania administration that, according to athletic department sources, Penn decided to undergo a self-imposed deemphasis, going from a 1979 Final Four Goliath to a floundering mid-1980s David.

So by 1989, when Princeton was matched against the nation's No. 1 ranked team, Georgetown, it would be the understatement of the century to say that expectations were low. As previously alluded to, the Ivy League's transmogrification from Goliath to David had mostly generated ridicule, not respect. Dan White's laudatory and visionary 1975 celebration of smart, intelligent Ivy League basketball had devolved into an outcry of "they don't belong here"! Even Dick Vitale was not a David fan at the time. However, on March 17, 1989, all of this was about to change.

On that night, the famed Princeton offense, and its counterpart stingy scoring defense, flustered and flummoxed Alonzo Mourning - arguably the nation's best player - and the dynastic Georgetown Hoyas. Poor shooting and minimal possessions led to impatience and frustration on Georgetown's part, leading ultimately to panic (the 1985 Villanova nightmare revisited?). It had been less than a decade since a group of college age U.S. Olympians shocked the Soviet Union hockey team. For Princeton - led by Bob Scrabis, Kit Mueller, Matt Lapin and George Leftwich - to defeat No. 1 ranked Georgetown would have resulted in a much more improbable upset; but it almost happened. The outcome wasn't determined until the final minute and even though Princeton lost the game, 50-49, the Tigers won the hearts of America. By the second half, the game, which was supposed to be a walkover, had basketball fans nationwide riveted to their TV screens. In one evening, Princeton had reprised its faded identity as "thinking" America's team. This game demonstrated "March Madness" at its most electrifying.

ESPN and Dick Vitale, who had lost interest in the Ivy League during the 1980s, now had rediscovered the charm of cerebral Princeton basketball. Pete Carril's disciplined "Princeton style" became the talk of the college basketball community. Coach Carril also became the darling of ESPN commentators, including Vitale and Digger Phelps. After the near upset of Georgetown, the Ivy League's 14 year old "David brand" had become fashionable overnight.

1989 was also the year that Fran Dunphy became the head coach at Penn. By 1994, what had become a dormant Penn program achieved a peak ranking of No. 11, led by Matt Maloney (Magnificent Eleven), Jerome Allen (Episcopal Academy) and Ira Bowman. In 1996 - Coach Carril's final season - his "disciplined David's" upset the defending national champion in the first round of the NCAA Tournament. Gabe Lewullis, Sydney Johnson and a young Steve Goodrich led Princeton to a 43-41 victory over UCLA (note the combined David-esque point total). Two years later in 1998, Goodrich, Lewullis and Mitch

Henderson achieved a 27-2 record and a peak ranking of No. 8 under Coach Bill Carmody. Therefore, between 1994 and 1998 both Penn and Princeton briefly revisited the vaunted "Goliath status" that had been their normalized condition during the post-Bradley Golden Age.

At length, as the attached Ivy League timeline displays, from the first college game between Yale and Penn in 1897 to Harvard's No. 21 ranking in 2012, the Ivy League has played a very important role in basketball history. As the actor, Kevin Costner (also a good friend of Columbia football player and actor, Brian Dennehy), proclaimed when discussing the legend of the Hatfields and the McCoys, "everyone thinks they know the story, but no one really does". The same can be said of the history of Ivy League basketball and, in particular, the post-Bill Bradley Golden Age (1964-1979). It was during this period that nationally-ranked Goliath teams and their NBA-caliber players roamed the hardcourt and were evenly matched against both ACC and Big Ten opponents. The proud legacy of these teams lives on to the current day and serves as a potential paradigm for the future of Ivy League basketball.

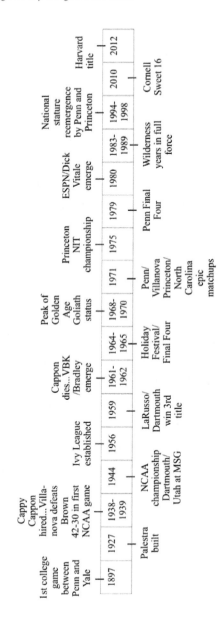

IVY LEAGUE BASKETBALL HISTORICAL TIMELINE

1897	1927	1938-1939	1944	1956	1959	1961-1962	1964-1965	1968-1970	1971	1975	1979	1980	1983-1989	1994-1998	2010	2012
1st college game between Penn and Yale	Palestra built	Cappy Cappon hired...Villanova defeats Brown 42-30 in first NCAA game	NCAA championship Dartmouth/Utah at MSG	Ivy League established	LaRusso/Dartmouth win 3rd title	Cappon dies...VBK/Bradley emerge	Holiday Festival/Final Four	Peak of Golden Age Goliath status	Penn/Villanova Princeton/North Carolina epic matchups	Princeton NIT championship	Penn Final Four	ESPN/Dick Vitale emerge	Wilderness years in full force	National stature reemergence by Penn and Princeton	Cornell Sweet 16	Harvard title

DAVID / GOLIATH-O-METER

IVY LEAGUE POWER CONFERENCE SCALE*

1965	1966	1967	1968	1969	1970	1971	1972	1973	1974	1975	1976	1977	1978	1979
8	7	8	10	10	10	10	10	8	7	8	7	6	7	7

SCALE RANKING
Strong Goliath = 8-10
Moderate Goliath = 6-7
David = <6

OTHER GOLIATHS
1959 = 6
1994-1996 = 6
1998 = 6
2010 = 6

*League-wide strength, between 1967-1973 Princeton/Penn/Columbia and Duke/North Carolina/Indiana were interchangeable basketball powers.

CHAPTER **9**

Six Degrees of Separation: The Golden Age Pantheon and the NBA Connection

> **Pop Culture Observation:** The following serves as testimony as to why the NBA could use more Ivy League-educated players such as Harvard's Jeremy Lin: "I don't know if the guys knew who he was... it came as a big shock to them when he was killed." **Los Angeles Lakers star Kobe Bryant, commenting on a team outing to see the movie "Lincoln".**

While the Golden Age heritage of NBA players (Magnificent Eleven plus Jeremy Lin) and coaches (VBK, Harter, et al) is memorable for those who lived through the era, the Golden Age connection to the NBA during its six decade existence (1946-2013) is equally fascinating. If one closely examines the record, there are numerous counterintuitive elements in NBA history that, on the surface, appear to be perplexing. For instance, the greatest and most significant basketball player of the Golden Age Era - and possibly of all-time - is Rick Barry...not Bill Bradley. Also, in terms of the greatest basketball players in NBA history, the college program that generated the most top 20 legends is LSU (a football school) not UCLA, Duke or North Carolina. In addition, this "Louisiana paradox" parallels the Ivy League from the standpoint of the historical timeline (1956-2013). Finally, as previously discussed, many of the greatest coaches in NBA history are former Ivy/Big 5 mentors from the Golden Age Era. In particular, the greatest team in history - the 1992 Olympic "Dream Team" - was led by Ivy League and NBA Hall of Fame coach, Chuck Daly.

In many respects, the Golden Age of Ivy League basketball is emblematic of "The History of the NBA" and, conversely, the history of the NBA is embodied in the Golden Age narrative. This narrative thread runs along a time-continuum from the first college game played between Penn and Yale in 1897, through the Golden Age (1964-1979), all the way to the 2012 NBA Finals featuring LeBron James and Kevin Durant.

In addition, the Golden Age tentacles spread out into the lives and careers of many of the greatest players in NBA history as well as many of the political and business leaders of contemporary America. The pantheon of Ivy stars, their legendary coaches and notable fans/classmates are the vessels through which these various connections are established.

In order to provide a road map of the threads, tentacles and vessels creating this connective tissue, it is first necessary to identify the greatest players in NBA history. In this regard, let's start with the identification of the 20 greatest (best/most talented?) players as determined by two separate sources...Bill Simmons "the ESPN Sports Guy" and yours truly.

The NBA Connection

Identifying the 20 greatest players in NBA history is tautologically an extremely subjective and slippery exercise; similar to defining what the meaning of "is" is. First, it is necessary to distinguish among the terms most talented, best and greatest in selecting the Top 20 players. Also, one should acknowledge the role of personal bias in selecting fan favorites.

As such, these categories could be defined as follows:

1) **Most Talented** - A player whose objective skills and athletic ability (physical gifts) are superior to others in the areas of scoring, rebounding, defense, and all-around basketball ability.

2) **Best** - A player with the requisite skills and talent (see #1 above) who is also able to apply them with affect...consistently, game in-game out, year in-year out in an overtly superior, Hall of Fame fashion.

3) **<u>Greatest</u>** - The rare Hall of Fame player who combines #1 and #2 above with a preternatural, uncanny (almost eerie) ability to come through "in the clutch" on the largest stage, and lead his team to victory. The player whose mere presence conveys an unbeatable quality, suggesting domination and defeat before the game even begins. Finally, the greatest is evocative of an otherworldly level of myth, legend, and iconography (Michael Jordan anyone?).

4) **<u>Fan Bias</u>** - We all have to admit it. Bill Simmons has his favorite players and I have mine.

Therefore, with the above constraints, limitations and caveats, the following are two versions of the Top 20 NBA players of all-time. I refer the reader to Mr. Simmons' definitive tome, "The Book of Basketball", for a full review and understanding of his comprehensive - as well as brilliant - analysis.

One obvious distinction between Mr. Simmons' Top 20 versus my Top 20 is that my Top 20 actually consists of 26 players. This is either a very clever or very duplicitous contrivance on my part but as author, I get to set the rules. Besides, the inability to "hold the line" at 20 merely demonstrates how difficult it is to distinguish among greatness.

As such, the following are comparative lists of the Top 20 greatest NBA players followed by their own unique connection to the Golden Age of Ivy League basketball:

Top 20 NBA Players of All-Time	
Bill Simmons (Selected in 2009)	Paul Hutter (Selected in 2013)
1. Michael Jordan	Kareem Abdul-Jabbar
2. Bill Russell	Michael Jordan
3. Kareem Abdul-Jabbar	Bill Russell
4. Magic Johnson	Magic Johnson
5. Larry Bird	Larry Bird
6. Wilt Chamberlain	Wilt Chamberlain / Kobe Bryant
7. Tim Duncan	Jerry West / Oscar Robertson
8. Jerry West	Shaquille O'Neal / Bill Walton
9. Oscar Robertson	Tim Duncan
10. Hakeem Olajuwon	LeBron James
11. Shaquille O'Neal	Hakeem Olajuwon / Moses Malone
12. Moses Malone	John Havlicek
13. John Havlicek	Julius Erving
14. Elgin Baylor	Elgin Baylor
15. Kobe Bryant	David Robinson
16. Julius Erving	Karl Malone

Top 20 NBA Players of All-Time	
Bill Simmons (Selected in 2009)	Paul Hutter (Selected in 2013)
17. Bob Pettit	Rick Barry
18. Karl Malone	Charles Barkley
19. Charles Barkley	Isiah Thomas / Walt Frazier
20. LeBron James	Kevin Durant / Bob Pettit
Special Category : <u>Most Talented</u>	
"Pistol Pete" Maravich	

The NBA Top 20 / Golden Age Connection

1) **Kareem Abdul-Jabbar** - Kareem's Golden Age connection begins but does not end with Hall of Fame teammates Magic Johnson and Bob McAdoo, who were two of the leading Ivy League antagonists during the Golden Age era. Magic vanquished Penn in the 1979 Final Four while McAdoo lost to Princeton in the Golden Age "Swan Song" battle in 1971. In addition, Kareem's Laker coach, Pat Riley, was Jim McMillian's teammate on the 1972 NBA champion Lakers team. Finally, UCLA was the "gold standard" throughout the Golden Age era and a UCLA player named Lew Alcindor was rated by ESPN to be the greatest college player of all-time. I wonder whatever happened to him?

2) **Michael Jordan** - MJ was a McDonald's All-American in the late Golden Age/incipient ESPN era. He was later a leader of the 1992 Olympic "Dream Team" (the greatest team ever assembled... even more talented than the 1968 Princeton Tigers) coached by Penn/Pistons Hall of Famer, Chuck Daly.

3) **Bill Russell** - As player/coach he beat VBK in the 1968, '69 NBA Finals. Also, as previously mentioned, a taller version of Jim McMillian.

4) **Magic Johnson** - See Kareem Abdul-Jabbar above. Also a member of Coach Daly's Dream Team. He was coached by McMillian's Lakers teammate, Pat Riley, during the 1980s "Showtime" era; and, of course, he defeated Penn in the 1979 Final Four.

5) **Larry Bird** - 1979 Final Four runner up, 1992 Dream Team member. Celtics teammate of Chris Ford (Villanova) and Bill Walton(Trailblazers/Dr. Jack Ramsay) who were both integral to the Ivy/Big 5 connection.

6) **Wilt Chamberlain / Kobe Bryant** - As the greatest players in Philadelphia history, the highest single game scorers in NBA history (100 and 81 points, respectively) as well as the best players on several of

the greatest teams in NBA history; both Wilt and Kobe deserve to be ranked at least #6 (if not higher). By the time Kobe retires, his career statistics will have surpassed Michael Jordan with only Kareem standing ahead of him. The bottom line is that Bill Simmons is from Boston and doesn't like Kobe, while I am from Philadelphia and I like Kobe (disclaimer: I played against his dad, Joe "Jellybean" Bryant, in high school, further enhancing my bias).

In terms of Golden Age connections, Kobe's dad played at Bartram High School (the same high school as Bill Bradley's Knick teammate, Earl "the Pearl" Monroe), at Big 5 La Salle College and then on the 1977 NBA finalist 76ers team (owned by Fitz Dixon...Episcopal Academy and Harvard). Joe Bryant and teammate, Julius Erving, lost that year to the Dr. Jack Ramsay/Bill Walton-led Trailblazers. Kobe Bryant played at suburban Lower Merion High School (not far from the Kobe Steakhouse) where he competed against the Inter-ac schools, particularly Episcopal, Haverford and Malvern Prep.

Wilt, of course, was coached by Butch van Breda Kolff in 1968 and was a 1972 Lakers teammate of Jim McMillian. Also, as Philadelphia schoolboy legends, both Wilt and Kobe played many high school tournament games at Penn's Palestra. Finally, the "six degrees of separation" focal point, Kevin Bacon, is from Philadelphia (Masterman Junior High) and is a fan of both Kobe and Wilt.

7) **Tim Duncan / David Robinson** - The most significant connection to the Golden Age is their style of play. The Tim Duncan/David Robinson Spurs displayed the same fluid teamwork that was the hallmark of the Golden Age era teams such as the Celtics, Lakers, Knicks, and Pete Carril's Princeton Tigers. The Spurs credo is: "no man moves more quickly than the ball". In 2013, the Spurs represent Golden Age/old school reincarnate.

8) **Oscar Robertson / Jerry West** - From college in the late-50s to the mid-70s, these bookend rivals had parallel careers. They were the All-American forerunners of Bill Bradley and NBA teammates of McMillian, Wilt, Kareem and Pat Riley.

9) **Shaquille O'Neal / Bill Walton** - At UCLA, Lew Alcindor was the greatest college player of the first half of the Golden Age (1964-1971) while Bill Walton was the greatest player of the second half of the Golden Age (1972-1979). As mentioned, Walton was the star of the Dr. Jack Ramsay coached,

1977 NBA champion Portland Trailblazers. Walton also teamed with Larry Bird and Kevin McHale on the greatest NBA team in history, the 1986 Boston Celtics. Finally, at Portland, he teamed with Princeton's Geoff Petrie before Petrie was forced into retirement due to chronic knee injuries.

Shaq was the last of the three LSU stars on the list of NBA Top 20 all-time greats (O'Neal, Maravich, Pettit). He was a McDonald's All-American who later teamed with Kobe Bryant to lead the NBA champion Lakers teams of the early 2000s.

10) **Julius Erving / Moses Malone / Rick Barry** - While Barry will be discussed separately, all three were critical to the rise of the ABA leading ultimately to the NBA/ABA merger in 1976. Barry and Erving provided the ABA with star power and credibility. Then a continuous flow of younger talent such as Moses Malone and Princeton's Brian Taylor followed. Dr. J and Taylor were the stars of the mid-70s New York Nets championship teams. Later, Dr. J and Moses Malone were the stars of the 1983 76ers NBA champions. This Fitz Dixon conceived 76ers team also included North Carolina's Bobby Jones.

11) **John Havlicek / Elgin Baylor / Bob Pettit** - Three great NBA stars during the early and peak years of the Golden Age. Baylor teamed with Wilt and Jerry West on van Breda Kolff's Lakers. Later he was replaced by Jim McMillian, a move that initiated the record 33 game win streak. Havlicek was Bill Russell's teammate during the 1960s and then led the Celtics to two NBA titles during the mid-1970s. Bob Pettit, one of the LSU legends, was the original power forward superstar. He was the prototype for Elvin Hayes, Karl Malone and Dirk Nowitzki, a great shooter and rebounder.

12) **Isiah Thomas / Walt Frazier** - Thomas was the leader of the Detroit Pistons who won back-to-back NBA championships in 1989 and 1990. Penn coaching legends Chuck Daly and Jack McClosky were the architects of these great Pistons teams. In addition, they were ably assisted by former Penn coach, Dick Harter. As a demonstration of the extent of the Ivy League/NBA coaching legacy, in 2012 former Jim McMillian Lakers teammate, and Lakers/Knicks coach, Pat Riley, was presented with the Chuck Daly Lifetime Achievement Award after his Miami Heat defeated Oklahoma City in the NBA Finals. It is arguable that, along with the Celtics' Red Auerbach and Bulls/Lakers' Phil Jackson, Penn/Pistons Coach

Daly is among the most significant coaches in basketball history. Of course, Walt Frazier was Bill Bradley's New York Knick counterpart.

13) **LeBron James / Kevin Durant** - Pat Riley's best Miami player, LeBron James, is moving up the ladder of all-time greats as is his primary contemporary rival, Kevin Durant. While LeBron is considered to be possibly the "most physically gifted" player in history, unless he continues to accumulate championship rings, he will have difficulty shaking his not-ready-for-prime-time reputation...stay tuned. Kevin Durant is the newest NBA superstar and given his current trajectory, he has ample opportunity to move up the Top 20 rankings scale. Durant was a "basketball country" high school prodigy from Washington D.C. He is on track to become a 30,000 plus career scorer, joining only Kareem Abdul-Jabbar, Karl Malone, Michael Jordan, Wilt Chamberlain and Kobe Bryant in that esteemed group. LeBron should eventually be there as well.

From a media standpoint, both Charles Barkley and Rick Barry's son, Jon, are high profile NBA analysts, dissecting the seasonal pursuits of LeBron and Durant.

Louisiana Paradox : Most Talented versus the Greatest

Just to completely confuse the issue among: the most talented, the most athletically gifted, the best and the greatest; I think it is timely to revisit a conundrum known as the "Louisiana Paradox", personified by the inimitable "Pistol Pete" Maravich. Maravich played at LSU during the height of the Golden Age, serving as a counterpoint to Lew Alcindor and the great UCLA dynasty in the years between 1968-1970. He averaged 44 PPG and was the leading scorer in NCAA history. He was also the best ballhandler/showman by far*...including Magic Johnson, Meadowlark Lemon, Curly Neal and the other Harlem Globetrotters. He did all of this before the advent of the three point line and, since many of his shots were from beyond 25 feet, he probably would have averaged 50 PPG in the post-ESPN era. In the NBA, his highest single game output was 68 points against the Knicks, again, without the advantage of the three point line.

However, even though he was ranked as the 5th greatest college player of all-time (just ahead of Bill Bradley), no one ever accused Maravich's LSU team (nor his NBA teams) of threatening to win a championship. He was a totally unique one-man-band, an exclusive category of which he was the only member. His skill-set was so individual that it bordered on Autistic (think "Rain Man" with a basketball). The bottom line is that no other human being could even think about doing the things that "Pistol Pete" could do with a basketball. In this regard, I believe it is fair to label Maravich the "most talented" player of all-time with LeBron James being the most "athletically gifted", Michael Jordan the "best" and Kareem Abdul-Jabbar the "greatest" at both the college (ESPN ranking) and NBA level.

Finally, an LSU/Golden Age father and son connection can be established between Pistol and his father, Press Maravich, and Butch van Breda Kolff and his son, Jan. Both Pistol Pete and Vanderbilt's Jan van Breda Kolff were Southeastern Conference players of the year, five years apart. In addition, both Butch VBK and Press Maravich were vagabond coaches of the "Evangelical Preacher" ilk who hailed from the great basketball state of Pennsylvania.

Rick Barry

When one daydreams of a Hawaiian vacation, one first ruminates about a brand and a perception. The mere thought process itself elicits a positive physical and emotional response...palm trees wafting in the late afternoon leeward breeze, as one contemplates ordering his or her first tropical cocktail of the evening. This is the physical/psychic translation of the "Hawaiian brand".

Similarly, when one thinks of Bill Bradley, the brand/perception mechanics kick in as people of a certain age conjure up memories of a great legend with a laundry list of accomplishments and attributes. However, if one closely examines the facts and details, it quickly becomes apparent that Rick Barry, and not Bill Bradley (or Kareem Abdul-Jabbar for that matter), was the most significant player to emerge from the Golden Age era.

The 1965 consensus All-American team was as follows:

- Bill Bradley - Princeton
- Rick Barry - Miami
- Billy Cunningham - North Carolina
- Dave Stallworth - Wichita State
- Gail Goodrich - UCLA
- Cazzie Russell - Michigan

Bradley was voted College Player of the Year by a wide margin. In addition, some considered him to be the greatest college player in history (again, until 1965 only Bill Russell, Oscar Robertson and Jerry West would have been under consideration for that honor). Rick Barry was the nation's leading scorer and beyond that he was considered to be "a good looking guy" and an afterthought... what is wrong with this picture?

In this segment I will make the case that 6'8" Rick Barry, not Bill Bradley, is the seminal player of the Golden Age. In addition, I will make the case that Rick Barry is the paramount figure in NBA history (1946-2013)...not Russell, Jordan, Wilt, Kareem, Magic or Bird. He was the heir to Bob Pettit, and the prototype for Larry Bird in the 1980s and LeBron James today.

1) **Rick Barry Versus Bill Bradley** - They both graduated in 1965, the same year that Bob Pettit retired. Bradley enrolled at Oxford and returned two years later to play for the Knicks beginning in 1967. After an underwhelming rookie season, he spent his summer playing in Philadelphia's Charles Baker Summer League retooling his game in order to become an effective combo-guard by the outset of the 1968-69 season.

This is what Rick Barry accomplished during the same time frame, even though the astute sports analysts at the New York media-complex (*New York Times/Sports Illustrated*) missed the significance of Barry's ability at the time of his graduation.

First, after leading the NCAA in scoring during his senior year (37.4 PPG versus Bradley's 30.6 PPG) he became an immediate NBA superstar for the Golden State Warriors in 1966. Forget mere rookie of the year honors. Barry averaged 25.7 PPG in his rookie season, then he broke Wilt Chamberlain's 8 year hold on the NBA Scoring Title by averaging 35.6 PPG in his second season. Also in his second year, he led the Warriors to the NBA Finals before losing to Wilt and the great 1967 76ers team. In 2012, ESPN made much of the fact that Oklahoma City's Russell Westbrook scored 43 points in the NBA Finals against LeBron James and the Heat...at age <u>23</u>!! For the record, Rick Barry scored 55 points in the NBA Finals against Wilt Chamberlain and the 76ers...at age 23!! In his third year Barry left the NBA to become the foundational superstar of the new ABA. This was a move that had a major impact on the history of professional basketball and still reverberates today. Barry did all of this before Bill Bradley even played his first game with the Knicks.

Barry shared Butch van Breda Kolff's abrasive personality and vagabond tendencies. His willingness to leave the NBA after becoming arguably its best player is almost unimaginable in its recklessness and/or courage. Meanwhile, Bradley joined the Knicks and he would remain with the franchise his entire career. His career represented a display of mature anti-vagabond tendencies as well as demonstrating a cosseted, cautious instinct...not to mention astute positioning for an eventual New Jersey senatorial campaign.

2) **Rick Barry Versus Don Nelson** - In 2012, longtime NBA coach Don Nelson was inducted into the Basketball Hall of Fame. In addition to his 45 year record as a player and coach, Nelson has been credited with developing the offensive innovation known as the "point-forward"; using a forward as a creator and distributor of the offensive flow outside the lane. Both Larry Bird and, currently, LeBron James are considered to be great point-forwards.

One problem with crediting Coach Nelson with the point-forward innovation is that he didn't even begin his coaching career until the late 1970s. This was several years after Barry led the Golden State Warriors to the 1975 NBA championship...<u>as a point-forward</u>! Rick Barry was the prototypical point-forward. His excellent passing ability, coupled with his deep outside shooting accuracy and 90% plus foul shooting make him arguably the most influential basketball player in history. As of 2013, the NBA game has evolved to where Rick Barry was in 1967: supreme point-forward skills (Bird, James), superlative outside shooting skills (Bird, Reggie Miller, Kevin Durant) and excellent foul shooting (Bird, Durant, Kobe Bryant).

Of the Top 20 NBA players of all-time, no one else has had this kind of impact on the game...not Kareem, Wilt, Walton, West, Oscar, Jordan, Shaq, Magic or Dr.

J. None of these superstars has had the innovative influence on basketball as it is played in 2013, that Rick Barry has had (possible exception, Dr. J.). On the contrary, great center play as demonstrated by Kareem, Wilt, Walton, Shaq, Patrick Ewing and Hakeem Olajuwon has become a lost art. (As a final insult, in 2013 the NBA eliminated the center position from All-Star voting and replaced it with the ignominious "front court player" designation).

4) **Rick Barry and the Golden Age Connection** - The Golden Age spanned from 1964-1979 (Bill Bradley to Tony Price). Rick Barry's NBA career spanned from 1965 to 1980 (Bill Bradley to Larry Bird). During this Golden Age-encompassing time span, Barry scored 25,279 points...more than any other player except Kareem Abdul-Jabbar. In addition, he was the foundational ABA superstar. More than any other player, he was responsible for the merger between the NBA and the ABA (again, possible exception, Dr. J.). His innovative point-forward offensive style was decades ahead of its time, and is replicated by today's superstars such as LeBron James, Kobe Bryant and Kevin Durant. Finally, and most important, his irascible, abrasive, highly competitive, impatient vagabond nature would be entirely compatible with the "Father of the Golden Age" himself, Butch van Breda Kolff...enough said.

4) **Rick Barry and the Media** - After his NBA career, Barry picked up the mantle of Princeton's Bud Palmer by becoming a CBS television commentator for NBA games. In recent years, Barry's son, Jon, has continued the tradition as one of ESPN's key NBA analysts. As such, the Barry family remains at the vanguard of NBA history; the son of the prototypical point-forward is now interviewing the heirs to that position... LeBron, Kobe and Durant.

The Golden Age of Ivy League basketball is just a small piece of the mosaic of basketball history. Yet the lesson of the Golden Age (GAIB = VBK + $ Bill x NYT) is that <u>perception is reality</u>...<u>brand is everything</u>!

Brand building (propaganda?) - advertising, publicity, hype, myth making, Q-quotient, legend promotion, iconography, deification, media support and projection - trumps hard, cold facts. A classic example of advertising/promotion creating illusion/delusion is illustrated by the fact that a gecko and a duck have become the ultimate symbols of financial strength and integrity for the insurance industry. The "Rock of Gibraltor" is so 20th century. In April of 1965, virtually all of the sports media, NBA scouts and so-called "sports cognoscenti" considered Bill Bradley to be a far superior player to Rick Barry. However, by October of 1967, prior to Bradley's first NBA game, Barry had accomplished the following :

- NBA Rookie of the Year...25.7 PPG
- NBA leading scorer...35.6 PPG
- 55 points in an NBA Finals game at age 23
- A superstardom/iconography so powerful that it supported the successful launching of a new league...the ABA.
- The establishment of a style of play (point-forward) that was the forerunner of Larry Bird, LeBron James and Kevin Durant. This changed the arc of the NBA game forever by leading to the eventual demise of the dominant center position.

Again, Barry accomplished all of this between April, 1965 and October, 1967. During this same time period, Bradley was studying political science at Oxford. Still, the Ivy League's Golden Age and "the legend of Bill Bradley" <u>have always been about much more than basketball</u>, as the facts and data pertaining to Rick Barry underscore.

A larger-than-life hero based upon myth and legend is what history recalls (Bill Bradley); not the under-reported statistics and accomplishments of a truly history-making performer (Rick Barry). In this regard, both Rick Barry and Butch van Breda Kolff share a similar fate. They are historic Golden Age figures who have been relegated to the ranks of "forgotten men" by others upon whom legends have been built. Yet, in the end it was the "Dollar Bill" legend based upon:

- Bill Bradley's superlative basketball skills and academic diligence,
- Butch van Breda Kolff's NBA coaching style combined with his vast recruiting skills,
- Hyped by the New York media-complex which built Bill Bradley and the Princeton program into a myth on the level of Paul Bunyon and his blue ox, Babe...that allowed the Golden Age of Ivy League basketball to flourish for the 15 years between 1964 and 1979.

The Golden Age of Ivy League basketball was a phenomenon. It was a "rise and fall" saga with dynamics similar to the rise and fall of the Roman Empire. Pre-Bradley (1940-1963) Indiana, North Carolina, Michigan and Duke were elite teams in power conferences. During the Golden Age (1964-1979) they remained so. Finally, befitting their elite stature, they still remain at the top of college basketball rankings today in 2013.

Quite the contrary, an odd and unique confluence of factors led to the rise of the Ivy League to power conference stature during the Golden Age. Its "reversion to the mean" was to be expected. Still, there are many positive and instructive lessons that are relevant for contemporary Ivy League basketball participants that can be gleaned via an understanding of "what happened then" and "how we got to now".

The Greatest Teams in NBA History*

The 1992 Olympic "Dream Team" was the greatest team of all-time. The following are the greatest teams in NBA history :

1) **1986 Boston Celtics**: Larry Bird, Kevin McHale, Robert Parish, Dennis Johnson, Danny Ainge, Bill Walton

2) **1996-98 Chicago Bulls**: Michael Jordan, Scottie Pippen, Dennis Rodman

3) **1972 Los Angeles Lakers**: Wilt Chamberlain, Jerry West, Gail Goodrich, <u>Jim McMillian</u>, Happy Hairston, Pat Riley, Flynn Robinson

4) **1985-87 Los Angeles Lakers**: Magic Johnson, Kareem Abdul-Jabbar, James Worthy, various

5) **1967 Philadelphia 76ers**: Wilt Chamberlain, Hal Greer, Chet Walker, Luke Jackson, Wali Jones, Billy Cunningham

6) **1983 Philadelphia 76ers**: Julius Erving, Moses Malone, Bobby Jones, Maurice Cheeks, Andrew Toney

7) **1960-69 Boston Celtics**: Bill Russell, John Havlicek, Sam Jones, Bob Cousy, Bill Sharman, Tom Heinsohn (the greatest dynasty)

8) **1991-93 Chicago Bulls**: Michael Jordan, Scottie Pippen, various

9) **2000-02 Los Angeles Lakers**: Shaquille O'Neal, Kobe Bryant, various

10) **<u>1970-73 New York Knicks</u>**: Walt Frazier, Willis Reed, Dave Debusschere, <u>Bill Bradley</u>, Earl Monroe, Jerry Lucas, Dick Barnett , Phil Jackson

11) **<u>1974-76 New York Nets</u>****: Julius "Dr. J" Erving, <u>Brian "BT" Taylor</u>, "Super" John Williamson, Larry "Special K" Kenon, Billy "the Whopper" Paultz, Billy "the Kid" Melchionni

Honorable Mention

1) 2003 San Antonio Spurs (David Robinson, Tim Duncan)

2) 1989-90 Detroit Pistons (Isiah Thomas, Joe Dumars)

3) 2007 Boston Celtics (Kevin Garnett, Paul Pierce, Ray Allen)

4) 1971 Milwaukee Bucks (Kareem Abdul-Jabbar, Oscar Robertson)

5) 1981-84 Boston Celtics (Larry Bird, Kevin McHale, Robert Parish)

6) 1977-78 Portland Trailblazers (Bill Walton, Lionel Hollins...coached by Dr. Jack Ramsay, University of Pennsylvania Ph.D.)

7) 2012-13 Miami Heat (LeBron James, Dwayne Wade)

---

*   Not only did Bill Bradley, Jim McMillian and Brian Taylor play on championship teams, but they played on some of the best teams in history.

**   In the ABA, "cool" nicknames were obligatory.

Lisa Delarosa

"King James"

Quotable

John Maynard Keynes on Winston Churchill's prodigious Nobel literary output pertaining to the history of war..."brilliant autobiography disguised as history".

Winston Churchill..."history will be kind to me for I intend to write it".

Ray Lewis/Baltimore Ravens..."when you believe what you believe, no matter what you believe, the ultimate is the ultimate".

Anonymous (1472 A.D.)..."there is a fine line between profundity and gibberish"...in anticipation of Ray Lewis' comments after winning the Super Bowl in 2013.

Confucius..."it is impossible to wake someone up who is pretending to be asleep".

Benito Mussolini, advertising executive..."it takes faith to move mountains because it gives the illusion that mountains can move. Illusion is perhaps the only reality in life".

Bibliography

Season of the 76ers (Wayne Lynch)

March Madness (John Wooden, Pete Newell)

The Official NBA Encyclopedia

Win at Any Cost (Francis X. Dealy)

Linsanity (Timothy Dalrymple)

My Life as a Sports Writer (Frank Deford)

The Last Lion: Defender of the Realm, 1940-1965 (William Manchester and Paul Reid)

Ivy Style (The Museum at FIT)

Something Like the Gods (Stephen Amidon)

Can I Keep My Jersey (Paul Shirley)

A Sense of Where You Are (John McPhee)

Exam Schools (Chester Finn and Jessica Hockett)

The Real Mad Men (Andrew Cracknell)

Memoirs of a Rugby Playing Man (Jay Atkinson)

My Cross to Bear (Gregg Allman and Alan Light)

History in the Making (J.H. Elliot)

The Ball (John Fox)

When the Game Changed (George Castle)

To Forgive Design ... Understanding Failure (Henry Petroski)

Aristocrats (Lawrence James)

Archives:

New York Times

Sports Illustrated

Philadelphia Inquirer

Philadelphia Daily News

New York Daily News

Princeton Alumni Weekly

Wall Street Journal

USA Today

New York Post

TedSilary.com

Acknowledgements

Special thanks to Bill Cronin and Ted Silary, without whom the completion of this book would have been impossible. Also, thanks to my wife, Marguerite Wagner, and my parents, Nancy and Joseph Hutter, as well as my family members Andrea and Hilary Hutter, for their patience and support. I appreciate the encouragement of my friends Dave Lawson, Jim Manley, Joe Gibbons, Russ Frank, Don Greif, George Ford, Chip Hall and Wighty Martindale.

Finally, a personal debt of gratitude to my research assistants, Lisa Delarosa and Ashley Tuccitto, whose talent and skill have made this project a success. Ditto to our project design artist, Constance Old.

About the Author

Paul Hutter was a young boy in Philadelphia during the 1960s. In addition to being an avid college and NBA fan, he played high school basketball at Germantown Academy (including several games at the Palestra). He attended countless Big 5 versus Regional Power games (Niagara/Calvin Murphy...UMass/Julius Erving, etc.) at the Palestra. He also attended Princeton University and commuted from Princeton to Manhattan after graduation in 1976.

During his high school years, and later as a member of Princeton's freshman basketball team, he either played with or competed against several of the players referred to in the book including: Geoff Petrie, Brian Taylor, Andy Rimol, John Berger, Fran Dunphy, Steve Bilsky, Dave Wohl, Jim Wolf, Ted Manakas, Barnes Hauptfuhrer, Ed Enoch, Jimmy Sullivan and Joe "Jellybean" Bryant. He was also "lightly recruited" by Penn (if dinner with "Digger" Phelps at Smokey Joe's qualifies for such a distinction). It is not true that Coach Phelps asked him to pick up the check.

Finally, he witnessed first-hand many of the key Ivy

League games during the Golden Age era including : Princeton/Michigan '64; Penn/Villanova '71; Princeton/North Carolina '71; Princeton's NIT victories in 1975 and Penn's NCAA Tournament games in 1979.

CPSIA information can be obtained at www.ICGtesting.com
Printed in the USA
BVOW10s0251071215

429558BV00014B/290/P